First Edition

triumphlearning™
Common Core Coach
English Language Arts
4

Common Core Coach, English Language Arts, First Edition, Grade 4   T103NA   ISBN-13: 978-1-61997-431-9
Cover Design: Q2A/Bill Smith   **Cover Illustration:** Jing Jing Tsong

Printed in the United States of America.   10 9 8 7 6 5 4 3 2

Contents

RL.4.2; RL.4.7; RL.4.9;
RL.4.10; RF.4.4.a, b; SL.4.1

RL.4.1; RL.4.2; RL.4.3; RL.4.4;
RL.4.6; RL.4.9; RL.4.10;
RF.4.4.a, b; SL.4.1; L.4.4.a

RF.4.4.c; W.4.3.a, b, d, e;
W.4.4; W.4.5; W.4.6; W.4.10;
L.4.1.f, g; L.4.2.a; L.4.4.a, c

RI.4.1; RI.4.2; RI.4.3; RI.4.5;
RI.4.6; RI.4.10; RF.4.4.a, b;
SL.4.1; L.4.4.b

**Common Core
State Standards**

W.4.3.a, c, e; W.4.4; W.4.5;
W.4.6; W.4.8; W.4.10; L.4.1.e;
L.4.2.d; L.4.3.b; L.4.5.c

RL.4.1; RL.4.2; RL.4.3; RL.4.5;
RL.4.10; RF.4.4.a, b; SL.4.1;
L.4.5.c

RL.4.1; RL.4.2; RL.4.4; RL.4.5;
RL.4.10; RF.4.4.a, b; SL.4.1;
L.4.5.a

W.4.1.a–d; W.4.4; W.4.5;
W.4.6; W.4.7; W.4.8; W.4.9.a;
W.4.10; L.4.1.b, c; L.4.3.c;
L.4.5.a, b

Reading Myths

Look at this erupting volcano in Hawaii. How do you think Hawaiians viewed volcanoes before scientists explained them?

ESSENTIAL QUESTION

How do myths help people understand the world around them?

Consider ▶ What forces of nature have shaped the Hawaiian Islands?

Why might people explain these forces with a myth?

Fires of Pele

adapted from a traditional Hawaiian myth

1   A time long ago, in a faraway land known as Kahiki, there lived a mother named Haumea and a father named Kanehoalani. Together they had seven sons and seven daughters. All of them were gods and goddesses. Whenever the clouds swelled and clung to the mountaintops, or rain fell, or the earth broke open and belched steam or fire, one of these powerful siblings had caused it.

One of the seven daughters was named Pele. She was the goddess of fire and volcanoes. She had learned much from the fire god Lonomakua. Pele had a terrible temper. Whenever she became angry or jealous, she would fly into a wild rage. If she stamped her feet, the ground would shake. If she cried, fiery lava would flow down the mountainsides. When she screamed or tossed her hair, the lava would shoot high into the air. Then it would rain down upon the valleys and the ocean below.

Pele didn't often stop to think about whether something seemed good or bad. She simply did whatever she felt like doing at that moment. This often brought her trouble. The fires she tended sometimes burned out of control. The fire that she rained down on the ocean sometimes burned the wooden canoes of the people who lived along the shore. This angered Pele's sister Makore. Makore was the goddess of the sea. When Makore herself was angry, she liked to show her displeasure by sending fearsome waves to break the canoes and pound them to splinters against the shore. But this was not the last time Pele would anger Makore.

MYTH A myth is often a story that explains something about the world and involves gods or superheroes. Myths usually explain how something in the world began or was created. What forces of nature are part of this myth?

THEME The theme of a story is the truth about life shown in that story. The beginning of this myth talks about Pele's anger. What truth about anger do you think the story may be suggesting?

Makore was older than Pele. She had taken notice of a strong, handsome warrior whom she had carried, this way and that, upon the waves she commanded. After some years, she admitted to him that she was in love with him. She then told her younger sister Pele about her feelings for the warrior. Pele wanted to see who had inspired Makore's love. When Pele saw him for herself, she too began to fall in love. Soon after, without considering Makore's feelings, Pele told the warrior that she loved him.

5   When Makore learned what Pele had done, she became enraged. She set out to chase Pele away from Kahiki forever. Pele quickly packed her things into a canoe her brother gave her. Then she paddled away from Kahiki as quickly as she could. She traveled for a long time, south and east across the warm Pacific Ocean, through the blinding brightness of day and the lonely darkness of night.

At last Pele reached the island of Kauai. There she rested for a while before choosing a mountain and climbing to the very top. There she took her digging stick and carefully carved a fire pit. She prepared to move into the pit and make it her new home.

But Pele's sister Makore had other plans. She followed Pele all the way to Kauai. She waited until Pele had finished digging the fire pit. Then Makore stirred up the ocean's waves. The waves splashed higher and higher, until they crested over the very top of the mountain. Pele's fire pit disappeared under water.

CONNECT TEXT AND ILLUSTRATIONS
Illustrations can be used to help readers imagine a scene, understand characters, or better grasp ideas in the text. How does the illustration on this page help you understand Pele's feelings as she sets out in her canoe?

PLOT The plot of a story is the sequence of events that includes the actions of the characters and a conflict. How do one character's actions make another character act in this story?

Pele was not discouraged when her fire pit was flooded. She slid down the mountain with her things and set out in her canoe once more. She forced her tired arms to paddle until she came ashore at the island of Oahu. Slowly, she climbed to the peak of a mountaintop there. Again she dug a large fire pit for herself.

Makore, still furious, was not so easily discouraged, either. She followed Pele to Oahu. When she saw the new pit Pele had dug, she stirred the sea again until waves flooded the mountaintop. For many days, Pele paddled patiently from island to island, with Makore pursuing her. From Oahu Pele went to Molokai, then to Lanai, and then to Maui. At each island, she would climb a mountain, dig a fire pit, and prepare to move in. Then her sister Makore would appear, sending enormous waves rolling at the mountainside. Each time, the pit was flooded, and Pele had to flee.

10 Finally, Pele landed on the "Big Island" of Hawaii. She climbed the mountain known as Kilauea. She found that she was very distant from the ocean waves. Her sister followed her to Hawaii and pushed the waves as high as she could. But Makore couldn't send the waves high enough or fast enough to wash to the top of Kilauea.

THEME Makore continues to chase Pele from island to island. Each time Pele digs a new fire pit, Makore floods and destroys it. The story describes how the two sisters' anger begins to change the Hawaiian Islands. How does this add to the theme of the story?

CONNECT TEXT AND ILLUSTRATIONS The map on this page shows the islands that Pele went to as Makore chased her. What features of the map connect to the details of the story?

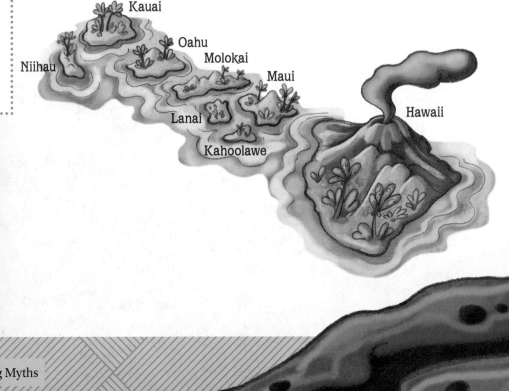

Kauai

Oahu

Molokai

Niihau

Maui

Lanai

Hawaii

Kahoolawe

At last Makore relented. She gave up her anger and slowly returned to Kahiki. No longer pursued by her sister, Pele settled into her fire pit on Kilauea, and there she stayed. But just as before, when Pele lost her temper, a roar could be heard as the ground rumbled. Hot lava shot high into the air. Then it flowed down the mountain as Pele screamed and tossed her hair.

That is how the Hawaiian Islands came to be the way they are. Pele, in retreat from Makore, would dig her mountaintop fire pit. Then Makore would push ocean waves at the mountain until the pit was filled with water. As they went along, the sisters left the story of their conflict behind them. It was forever carved into the rocks.

If you visit the island of Hawaii today, you can go to Kapoho and look for Green Mountain. Green Mountain holds an old pit—a volcanic crater. The crater is filled with water. If you visit Kilauea, where Pele resides, you can still hear a roar. You can feel rumbling beneath you. You can see the lava explode into the air and flow down the mountain slopes. As you watch and listen to the earth stir, you may tell yourself that Pele has once more lost her temper.

THEME In this story, the theme is that anger can have lasting effects. Stories can have more than one theme or message. What other message about anger is in this story?

SUMMARIZE A good summary states only the most important details of a story. *Two sisters who were goddesses were angry. One sister chased the other from island to island. As they went, they shaped the mountains as they still are today.* How would you summarize the story?

MYTH The purpose of this myth is to explain how the volcanoes of Hawaii were shaped. Why do you think this story was important to people who lived in Hawaii long ago?

Consider ▶ How does a myth in graphic form differ from a traditional telling of a myth?

How are the gods and goddesses in myths like real people?

Like Fire and Water!

CONNECT TEXT AND ILLUSTRATIONS
This version of the story is a graphic novel. Most of the story is told through illustrations and dialogue. The illustrations on this page show Makore and her mother. How does this version help you understand why Makore acts the way she does?

COMPARE PLOT
In this part of the plot, Makore and her mother talk about Pele's anger. How does this differ from the events in the first version?

The ground is shaking. Makore, have you said something to upset Pele?

She went to Aukelenuiaiku, saying she loved him. I will never forgive her!

Pele always gets exactly what she wants. But I'm not giving in this time! She'll be sorry.

Wait. I will talk with Pele. She is young and even more hot-tempered than you!

COMPARE PLOT In both versions of the story, Pele gets the canoe from her brother. But in this version, the plot includes different details about Makore and her brother. What details are included here that were not in the first version of the story? How do those details help you understand the characters?

CONNECT TEXT AND ILLUSTRATIONS In the first version of the story, Pele uses a digging stick to dig her fire pit. Compare that description with the illustration and dialogue at the top of this page. How is this version different? How does it add to your understanding of the story?

COMPARE PLOT Unlike the first version, this version of the story includes dialogue between Pele and Makore. How does that make the story different?

Pele paddled and paddled. She landed on Kauai, Oahu, and Molokai. Still Makore followed her, flooding each new home. But soon, Pele would find an island large enough to protect her.

Now forgive me and leave me in peace, Makore!

I will leave, Pele . . . but don't ever return to Kahiki!

Pele had found her new home. She remained forever sad that she could not return to the home of her birth, and she still grumbles and weeps tears of fire to this day.

COMPARE THEME

In the first version of the story, the theme focuses on how anger can have lasting effects. This version focuses more on the relationship between Pele and Makore. How does this make the theme of the graphic novel different?

COMPARE PLOT

The ending of the first story tells what you might experience if you visit Kilauea. The graphic novel ends with Pele alone on the mountain. How are the endings in the two versions different? How are they the same?

Comprehension Check

Look back at "Fires of Pele" and "Like Fire and Water!" How are the theme, plot, and structure different in the two stories? How are they the same? Use the Venn diagram below to list your ideas. In the center, write what is the same in both stories. On the sides, list what is different in the stories.

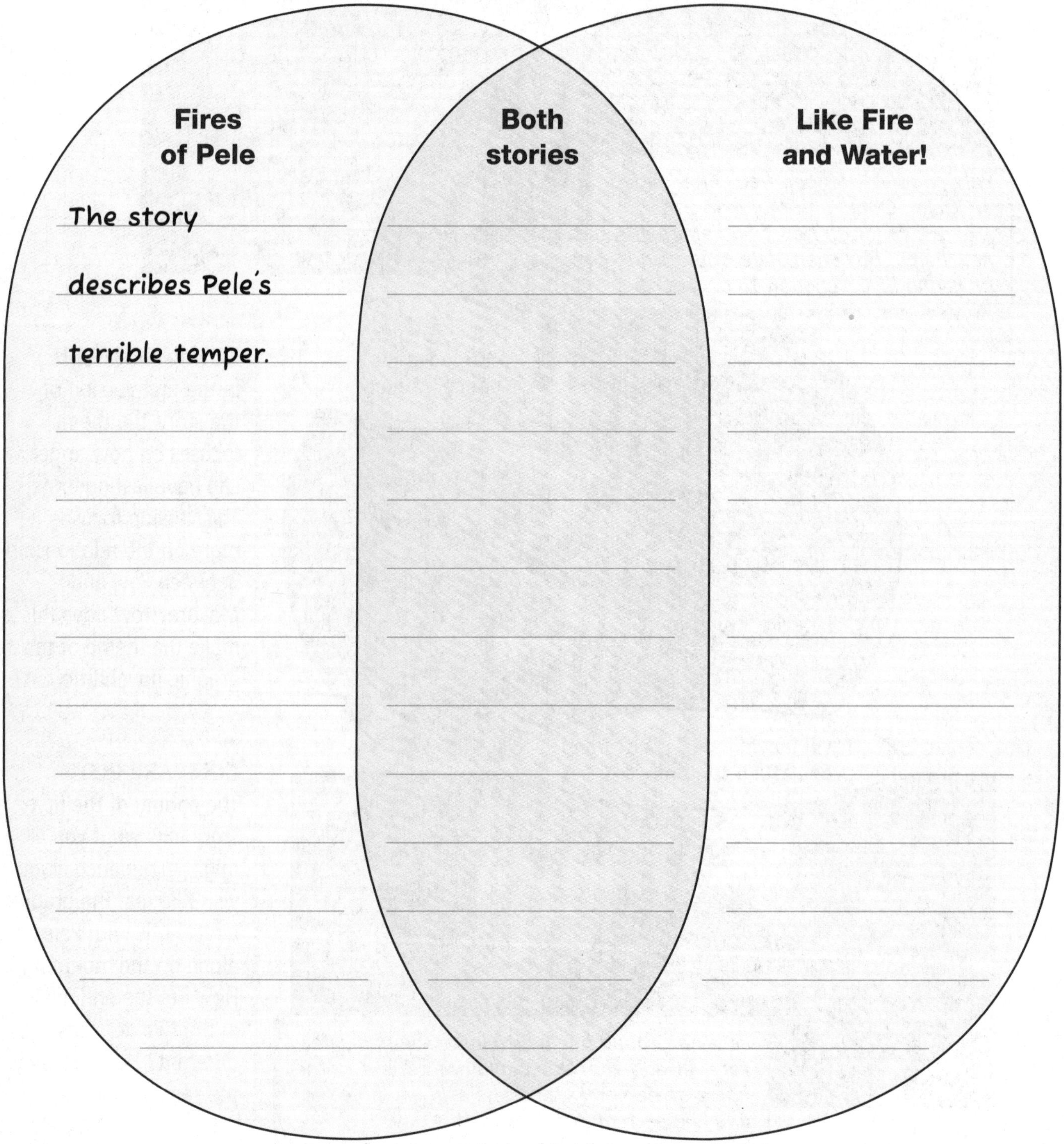

Fires of Pele

The story describes Pele's terrible temper.

Both stories

Like Fire and Water!

Vocabulary

Use the word map below to help you define and use one of the highlighted vocabulary words from the Share and Learn reading or another word your teacher assigns you.

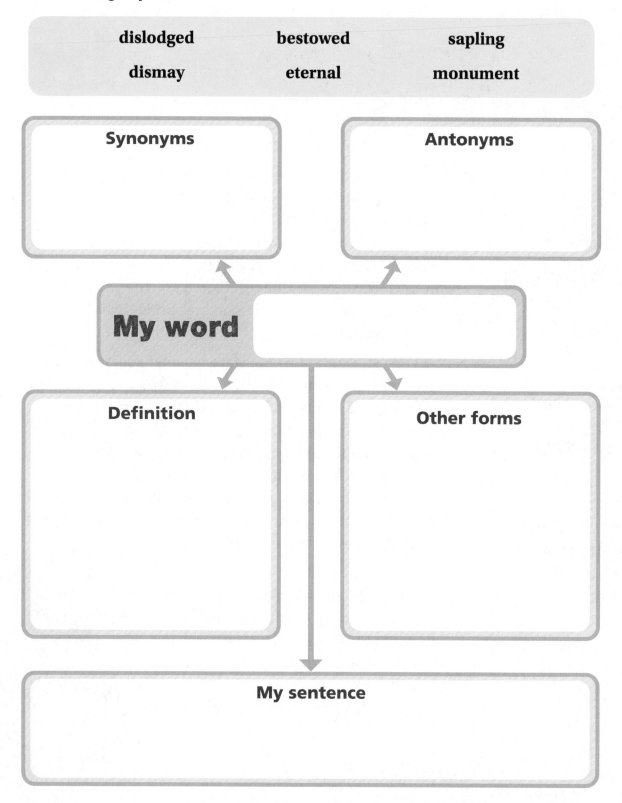

dislodged   bestowed   sapling

dismay   eternal   monument

Synonyms

Antonyms

My word

Definition

Other forms

My sentence

Consider ▶ How is the world of myths different from the real world?

Why do myths sometimes include angry or destructive actions?

Bridge of Fire

adapted from a Puyallup myth

1   Long ago, along the steep banks of the Columbia River, a pile of giant rocks was dislodged from the earth and tumbled into the water. There, the rocks created a bridge of stone. This bridge allowed the people to cross the river easily. Their feet stayed dry. There was no danger of being swept downstream by the rushing waters. The people loved the bridge. They named it Tamanawas Bridge, which means "Bridge of the Gods."

For a long time, the people were thankful for the bridge. They felt as if a great gift had been bestowed upon them. And the bridge led to many other gifts. Using the bridge, people could easily seek plants, trees, and animals on both sides of the river. People from one side of the river would cross the bridge to look for rare stones. People from the other side would cross to cut strong, straight saplings, the young trees they used to build their camps. Then each group would cross the bridge again to return to their homes.

But as time passed, people on each side of the bridge began to grumble. They complained about the things people across the river were taking away. One began to accuse the other, saying, "You are taking things from our side of the bridge! You must find them on your own side!"

"But you take from our side of the bridge, also!" the others would respond. "The bridge serves each of us. What I find across it, I may keep. After all, who has the right to claim the gifts of the earth as their own? How can things be yours after they have been cut or carried by another?" The arguments grew worse. Soon, everyone was fighting. They fought about the bridge, the land around it, and just about everything upon the land.

5   The Great Spirit Tyee Sahale watched with **dismay**. He grew sad and angry that the people were fighting with their neighbors. He decided that he must punish all of the people for their greediness. He thought about it for a long time. Finally, he caused all the fires in their homes to go out. There was only one way for people to light their fires again. They would have to travel to the one fire that still burned. Tyee Sahale placed this fire in the middle of the Bridge of the Gods.

A very old woman named Loowitlatkla, or "Lady of Fire," lived on the bridge. It was her job to look after the sacred fire. She was devoted to it. Night and day, Loowit worked to keep the fire going. Usually she added a handful of wood. If wood was scarce, she would use dry moss or anything else she could find to feed the fire.

COMPARE THEME
In "Fires of Pele," the theme was that anger can have a lasting effect. How is the theme of this story similar?

_____

_____

_____

CHARACTER
What kind of character is Tyee Sahale? Why does he decide to punish the people?

_____

_____

_____

CONTEXT CLUES
Circle the words that help explain the meaning of dismay.

THEME How does Loowit's hard work and kindness connect to the theme that anger and greed cause destruction?

_____

_____

_____

CONNECT TEXT AND ILLUSTRATIONS
Look at the illustration of Loowit. What do you learn about Loowit from the illustration?

_____

_____

Sometimes Loowit heard thunder or felt a sudden cool breeze. Then she would build the fire very high. That way any coming rain would not extinguish it. She always began to worry when the fire's flames burned low.

Loowit knew that the fire she tended was vital to the people. How would they stay warm at night or cook a meal without their fires? So Loowit was always kind to those who came to her for some of the fire's glowing embers. Although her back was bent and her hands were hard and worn, she would greet each visitor warmly. She always sent them home with hot coals and her good wishes.

Loowit's hard work and kindness caught the attention of Tyee Sahale. He could see that her back hurt and her hands ached. He wanted to give her something that would please her. He offered Loowit the gift of eternal life as a special reward for her efforts and her good nature. He had already given this same gift to his sons, Klickitat and Wyeast.

10   Tyee Sahale gave eternal life to Loowit, only to find that she did not want it. She did not want to be an old woman forever. But Tyee Sahale could not take back the gift he had given. He told Loowit he would grant her one wish. Loowit quickly wished to be full of youth and beauty again. Instantly she became a fair young woman.

Soon the news of Loowit's wondrous beauty had travelled across the land. Tyee Sahale's sons, the brothers Wyeast and Klickitat, were both curious to see Loowit for themselves. They both set out for the bridge. Wyeast came from the south. Klickitat stomped down from the north. The brothers arrived at the Bridge of Fire at the same time. Both of them instantly fell in love with Loowit.

Loowit was not used to having handsome young men pursue her. She did not want to cause any trouble between the brothers. When Klickitat and Wyeast each offered their love to her, she refused to choose between them. The brothers each believed that he alone could win Loowit's favor. They began a long and terrible battle.

They argued about which of them should be allowed to marry the beautiful Loowit. They stomped their feet and set fire to villages. The fires they lit burned out of control. Entire forests were swallowed by the flames. The people living in the river valley fled in terror. They never resolved their disagreements over the bridge.

CHARACTER What kind of person is Loowit? Why does she refuse to choose one of the brothers?

_____

_____

_____

FIGURATIVE LANGUAGE Explain the meaning of "entire forests were swallowed by the flames."

_____

_____

_____

PLOT The people had to leave the river valley. How did their actions earlier in the story cause this to happen?

_____

_____

_____

COMPARE MYTHS
Reread the last paragraph. How are the volcanoes in this myth similar to the volcanoes in "Fires of Pele"?

_____

_____

_____

Tyee Sahale saw all of the destruction caused by his sons. He became angrier than before. In a fit of temper, he struck the Bridge of the Gods. The bridge tumbled into the river, where it still lies. So angry was Tyee Sahale that he destroyed the three people to whom he had given eternal life—Loowit, Klickitat, and Wyeast.

15   After Tyee Sahale had punished them and the world fell silent, he felt great sorrow. He decided that he would make a monument to each of them. Where each suitor had fallen, he pushed the ground up to form a volcano.

Loowit had been beautiful. Where she had fallen, Tyee Sahale raised a volcano covered with glittering white snow. This is Mount St. Helens. Where Wyeast fell, Mount Hood stands tall and proud. Klickitat, so much in love with Loowit, still weeps for her, his head hanging sorrowfully in the form of Mount Adams.

Mount St. Helens

This myth explains the origin of three volcanoes in the Pacific Northwest. Mount St. Helens and Mount Adams are in what is now Washington State. Mount Hood is near them in Oregon.

Mount Adams

Mount Hood

SUMMARIZE
Summarize the story by retelling only the most important ideas in your own words.

_____

_____

_____

Anchor Standard Discussion Questions

Discuss the following questions with your peer group. Then record your answers in the space provided.

1. How do the characters in the myths "Bridge of Fire" and "Fires of Pele" view nature? Support your opinions with examples from each text.

_____

_____

_____

_____

_____

2. How would you represent Loowit's kindness in a graphic novel? Using a scene of your choice from "Bridge of Fire," create four panels that help readers better understand the goodness of her heart. Create your own dialogue and illustrations, and be prepared to support them with details from the text.

Comprehension Check

1. How does the characters' anger lead to problems in the plot of both "Fires of Pele" and "Bridge of Fire"?

_____

_____

_____

2. How are the themes, or messages, about life in "Fires of Pele" and "Bridge of Fire" the same? How are they different?

_____

_____

_____

3. Think about the endings of "Fires of Pele," "Like Fire and Water!" and "Bridge of Fire." Tell which ending you think is most hopeful, and why.

_____

_____

_____

Read On Your Own

Read another myth, "How Night Came," independently. Apply what you learned in this lesson and check your understanding.

Reading Short Stories

Look at this photograph of a shipwreck in the ocean. If you wanted to tell a story about an underwater adventure, how would you begin?

ESSENTIAL QUESTION

What can short stories teach us about the world we live in?

Consider ▶ Why is it important to understand the ocean's mysteries?

How can a short story explain information about the natural world?

Secrets of the Sea

1 Dr. Abbott, an ocean scientist, sent a question deep into the sea: "Dr. Lopez, can you hear me?" Dr. Lopez adjusted the volume on her headset. She moved the microphone closer.

"Yes, Dr. Abbott. Everything is fine down here. All systems are running smoothly."

Dr. Lopez studied the blinking depth chart on her monitor. She was inside a submersible, or deep-sea vehicle, six hundred meters below the surface of the ocean. The monitor screen provided the only light in the cabin. Even the red lights on the control panel had been turned off. Dr. Lopez knew the controls so well she could operate them in the dark.

Dr. Abbott also knew the controls well. For eight long years he had designed and redesigned the submersible, called *The Explorer*. He had created a vehicle that could withstand thousands of tons of water pressure. By rights, he should have been the one navigating it, not Dr. Lopez. But Dr. Abbott had failed the most critical test. He could not stand living underwater for very long. He had tried but had to give up after only two days. So there he was, in a research boat bobbing on the surface, watching a tiny computer screen. Dr. Lopez would get all the glory.

SHORT STORY A short story is a made-up tale with characters, a setting, and a plot. It is usually short enough to read in one sitting. As you read, look for details that indicate that this story is fiction.

SETTING The setting is where and when the story takes place. Authors usually use vivid descriptions to make the setting interesting. What is the setting of this story?

5   The team of scientists had an urgent goal. They hoped to find the most elusive and secretive animal of the sea— the giant squid. No human being had ever seen a live giant squid. On rare occasions, a dead squid would wash up on a beach somewhere in the world. Those giants were more than thirty meters! Their eyes were as big as volley balls!

For years, Dr. Lopez and Dr. Abbott had searched for the giant squid, with no luck. Now the scientists hoped their luck would change. Dr. Abbott had invented an entirely new kind of submersible, designed to dive deeper and stay down longer. It was more comfortable, too. Dr. Lopez could stand up, walk around, and even exercise. When she wanted to sleep, a robot could navigate the vehicle. She had been in *The Explorer* for a week already. It was beginning to feel like a second home.

For Dr. Lopez, finding a live giant squid had been a life-long search, a personal quest. As a child she had read myths about the giant squid. A myth from ancient Greece told of Hercules, the strongest man in the world. The gods tested Hercules's strength by making him wrestle with a giant sea serpent. The serpent, called a Hydra, had many arms, like a giant squid. Myths like that one made Dr. Lopez want to become an ocean scientist and discover the truth about this mysterious creature.

CONTEXT CLUES
Context clues are words located near an unknown word that can help you figure out what a word means. The word *elusive* is used along with the word *secretive* to describe the giant squid. The text also says that no one had ever seen a live giant squid. From these clues, what do you think *elusive* means?

CHARACTER Characters are the people who take part in the action of a story. They can be realistic or not. Often, a story includes major and minor characters. Which two characters are introduced so far in the story? What do you know about each character?

MAKE INFERENCES
An inference is a guess based on evidence. You can use details in the story to figure out something that's not stated directly. We read that Dr. Lopez is able to live in the submersible for a week and feels at home there. What inference can you make about what kind of person she is?

THE EXPLORER

SETTING What additional details do you learn about the setting of this story?

MAKE INFERENCES Sometimes information is left out to create suspense. What does the sighting of hoki mean for the scientists?

Down, down the submersible sank, deep into the dark ocean. Seven hundred meters, 800 meters. Most scientists thought giant squid lived at 650 to 2,600 meters. Dr. Lopez suspected that the creatures might hide at even greater depths.

When *The Explorer* reached one thousand meters, Dr. Lopez flicked on the spotlights. Suddenly the ocean came alive with hundreds of fish. Pearlsides zipped past the window. They were little fish, no bigger than her finger. Rows of lights glowed along their sides like tiny pearls. Lantern fish also darted back and forth, their big eyes shining in the submersible's spotlight.

10 "What can you see, Dr. Lopez?" asked Dr. Abbott.

"I see lots of fish, but nothing big enough to satisfy the giant we're after," Dr. Lopez answered. "I'll turn on the cameras now."

On the surface far above, Dr. Abbott and the research team gathered to watch images from *The Explorer*'s cameras. Dr. Abbott felt annoyed to be so far away from the action.

The scientists waited, watching the screen. A few silvery hoki passed by. The hoki were nearly a meter long—a tasty appetizer for a giant squid.

Suddenly, Dr. Lopez heard a loud clicking noise.

15 "Shhh," she said. "Listen. I've turned on the outside microphone."

Dr. Abbott and the team turned up the radio volume. They heard a series of fast clicks, then a few slow ones. The clicks grew louder. It sounded as if someone were tapping on the bottom of an empty can. The louder clicks sounded like small explosions.

"That's a sperm whale!" Dr. Lopez exclaimed. "Their voices carry a long way in the water. I'm guessing it's about a mile away. I'll navigate toward it now."

"Sperm whales prey on giant squid," said Dr. Abbott excitedly to the crew. "We don't know how they find the squid when we scientists can't. If there's a sperm whale down there, there might be a squid nearby."

They listened attentively as the whale's rapid clicks grew louder.

20   Suddenly, a huge brownish-gray body filled *The Explorer*'s window.

"Whale ahoy!" shouted Dr. Lopez. She maneuvered the camera just in time, carefully controlling the powerful lens. A magnificent sperm whale swam past. Suddenly the whale turned, displaying a pale underbelly. Long gray streaks ran along the belly.

"Wow!" Dr. Lopez cried. "A giant squid made those marks with the suckers on its tentacles!"

MAKE INFERENCES
We read that the scientists use the sounds they hear to identify the whale before they see it. What can you infer about their background knowledge of life in the ocean?

CONTEXT CLUES Look at the word *maneuvered*. If you don't know what the word means, look at the words around it. The words *carefully controlling* are context clues. What do you think *maneuvered* means?

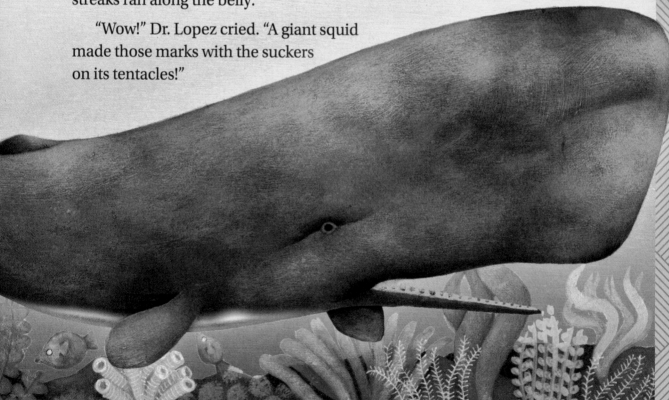

"Yes, that's their telltale sign," agreed Dr. Abbott. "That giant must have been a delicious lunch for the whale."

Dr. Lopez did not say anything, but she disagreed with Dr. Abbott. She felt strongly that the squid had escaped. The sucker marks were so long and deep, there must have been a Herculean struggle.

25 The sperm whale seemed curious about the submersible. It swam back and forth several times, as if wondering what this odd mechanical creature might be. Then it turned and disappeared in the dark water.

Dr. Lopez took a deep breath. Her hands trembled with excitement as she maneuvered the controls. At 3,015 meters, *The Explorer* gently bumped against the ocean floor.

"Dr. Abbott, I've reached the ocean floor. I'm going to move along the bottom for a bit. I feel we're close to something."

Dr. Abbott replied sternly, "No, this expedition is over. We're not going to find a live squid this time. Please begin *The Explorer*'s ascent to the surface."

Silence.

30 "Dr. Lopez?" Dr. Abbott called. The radio line crackled with static, followed by more silence.

Finally, a breathless voice came from 3,000 meters below.

"I see it, I see it!" exclaimed Dr. Lopez. "It's right in front of me! The instrument panel measures it at seventeen meters. It's bigger than a city bus!"

Seconds later, there it was on the video screen: a giant squid! Its eight arms and two long feeding tentacles danced in the water, as if waving at the crew. The strange balloon-like body expanded and contracted. It seemed more like a mythological creature than a real animal. As they watched, one of the long tentacles reached out and grabbed a hoki. They gasped. No humans on Earth had ever witnessed this before!

"Look at the eyes!" Dr. Lopez called. "They're bigger than my head! And those tentacles are at least ten meters long! This is it!"

35 Dr. Lopez could hear the team cheering far above her. His resentment forgotten, Dr. Abbott cheered as loudly as the others.

POINT OF VIEW Point of view is the author's choice of narrator or speaker. Point of view shows who is telling the story. In third-person point of view, the author, not a character, tells the story. The author uses the pronouns *he*, *she*, and *they*. What does the author tell the reader about the thoughts and feelings of the characters in this story?

CHARACTER Earlier in the story, Dr. Abbott was jealous because Dr. Lopez—and not he—was navigating *The Explorer*. At the end of the story, Dr. Abbott cheers as loudly as the others. This detail shows that his feelings have changed. How would you describe how Dr. Abbott's feelings have changed?

Consider ▶ How does first-person point of view in a story differ from third-person point of view?

How does a writer build suspense in a mystery story?

SETTING A setting can include details about weather, buildings, or objects. The author may include details that appeal to the five senses: sight, smell, hearing, touch, or taste. What is the setting at the beginning of this story? Why is this a good setting for the start of a mystery story?

POINT OF VIEW In the first-person point of view, the narrator is a character in the story. The narrator tells the story using the pronoun *I*. Who is the narrator in the story?

CONTEXT CLUES Find the word *steerage*. The phrase "crowded in the lowest rooms of a ship" may help you figure out its meaning. What do you think *steerage* means?

A Monumental Mystery

1   Click! The door to the attic softly closed. Trapped! How long could we survive without food and water? My imagination was off and running.

Nathan sneezed. "Sure is a lot of dusty old stuff up here, Ernesto," he said.

Nathan is my best friend and a cool dude. We were in Nathan's attic on a rainy Saturday morning, looking for family papers for a school project on immigration. Mr. Chou, our teacher, had suggested that some of us might have ancestors who had passed through New York City when they immigrated to the United States. Those relatives might have kept diaries or written letters that mentioned seeing the world-famous monument the Statue of Liberty.

I knew there weren't any papers like that at my house. My *abuela*, my grandmother, arrived in the United States on a plane to Miami, Florida. But Mrs. Edelstein, Nathan's mom, got all excited when we told her about the project.

5   "Nathan's great-great-great-uncle Harry was the first Edelstein to come over from Russia, in 1876," she said. "Uncle Harry was a poor cobbler, so he traveled in steerage, crowded in the lowest rooms of a ship with dozens of other passengers. He wrote lots of letters to his mother back in Russia. They're in the attic. Look in the third file cabinet on the left, top drawer. It's a heavy box, so be careful."

Statue of Liberty Time Line

1875 Sculptor Frédéric-Auguste Bartholdi begins construction of the statue in France, hoping it will be ready by 1876, the one hundredth anniversary of the Declaration of Independence.

1876 Bartholdi, behind schedule, sends what he has finished to the United States: the completed right hand and torch. They are displayed at the Centennial Exposition in Philadelphia and later in New York City before being returned to France.

It didn't take us long to locate the file cabinet at the back of the attic. Nathan opened the top drawer and struggled to remove a heavy box. Suddenly it slipped from his hands and fell, landing with a thud on an old sewing machine.

"What's in that box?" I wondered. "Bones?"

"Don't be silly, Ernesto," said Nathan, laughing. "But it feels heavy enough. Maybe it's a whole bunch of skeletons. Mom was right. Great-uncle Harry is heavy. Let's haul him downstairs."

We carried the box down to Nathan's room and set it carefully on his bed. The box was made of thick cardboard, worn smooth at the corners. A small brass latch was mounted on the front, and under it a label: "Papers of Harold Edelstein, 1876–1883." The glue on the label looked dry and cracked.

10   "Maybe there's gold inside," I whispered.

Nathan opened the latch. At first we were disappointed. The box was crammed with musty old magazine and newspaper clippings. But behind the other papers was a packet of pale blue envelopes, tied with a narrow ribbon. Nathan slid an envelope out of the packet and opened it carefully. I looked over his shoulder. The letter paper seemed as brittle and delicate as a moth's wing. At the top of the page, we could read the year: 1876!

That's all we could decipher. The cursive writing was in a foreign language, with strange backward letters and accents.

MAKE INFERENCES

Sometimes an author doesn't come right out and tell you everything about a character, a setting, or an event. The author expects the reader to connect the details to make inferences. In this story, Ernesto imagines they are trapped in the attic. Then he wonders if there are bones or gold in the box. These details provide evidence about Ernesto's character. What inference can you make about Ernesto from these details?

1885
The 214 separate parts of Liberty arrive in the United States in wooden crates.

1886
The assembled monument is dedicated in Upper New York Bay.

"Looks like a secret code," I suggested.

"Mom or Dad can make sense of this," said Nathan.

15 Mrs. Edelstein was at the computer in the kitchen, checking her e-mail.

"How's Great-uncle Harry?" she asked.

"Not so great," said Nathan. "We found his letters, but we can't read them. It must be a different language."

We showed Nathan's mother the letter with its strange writing.

"Oh, I should have remembered!" exclaimed Mrs. Edelstein. "He wrote to his mother in Russian, of course! Mrs. Genkina next door might be willing to translate the letters. She's from Russia."

20 After lunch, we called Mrs. Genkina and took the letters to her house. Her eyes opened wide when she saw them, as if they really were gold. She began to translate the first letter aloud.

> *"My Dearest Mama,*
>
> *It is a windy day here on the ship. I am terribly seasick and America seems far away . . ."*

Nathan interrupted her. "Could you please skim through the letters and just see if there are any references to the Statue of Liberty?" he asked politely.

Good old Nathan. He remembered our deadline. Mr. Chou said we had to complete a first draft of the report by Monday.

Mrs. Genkina didn't seem to mind being interrupted.

"Let's see." She paused. "Hmm . . . 1876. I'm sorry, boys. The Statue of Liberty wasn't completed until after these letters were written. I don't think you'll find any references here."

25 But she continued to skim through the letters. Suddenly, she stopped at one of them.

"Hold on, I'm wrong. Listen to this." she said.

"*'I saw part of the famous Miss Liberty in New York City this week,'*" Mrs. Genkina translated. "*'Her right hand is monumental. It is more than sixteen feet tall! I hope that someday in the future I will see all of her.'*"

Part of Miss Liberty? Her right hand? What did Great-uncle Harry mean?

Nathan snapped his fingers. "Let's find the answer online!" he said. "Thanks a lot, Mrs. Genkina!"

30 We raced back to Nathan's house. A quick computer search solved the mystery. We found a time line that showed important dates for the famous monument. The Statue of Liberty was supposed to be completed in 1876, but the French sculptor got behind schedule. So he sent over from France the two parts he had finished: Miss Liberty's right hand and her torch. That was the monumental hand Harry Edelstein saw in 1876!

POINT OF VIEW First-person point of view reveals only one character's experiences and feelings. Third-person point of view reveals information about all the characters. What kinds of information did you learn about the main characters in "Secrets of the Sea" that you don't learn about all the characters in this story?

PLOT A plot includes a conflict and a resolution. What is the main conflict in the story? How do the characters solve it?

SUMMARIZE A good summary states only the most important details of a story. How would you summarize this story?

Comprehension Check

In the story "A Monumental Mystery," the author presents a series of problems to solve. Each problem and solution moves the plot forward. The problems are listed below. Look back at the story, and fill in the solution for each problem. Then add details about the solution.

Problem	Solution	Solution Details
A. Ernesto and Nathan need to find family papers for a school project.	They find Great-uncle Harry's letters in the attic.	The box is heavy. Nathan drops it.
B. Harry Edelstein's letters are written in a foreign language.		
C. They need to find a reference to the Statue of Liberty.		
D. The boys don't understand why Great-uncle Harry saw only the statue's hand.		

Vocabulary

Use the word map below to help you define and use one of the highlighted vocabulary words from the Share and Learn reading or another word your teacher assigns you.

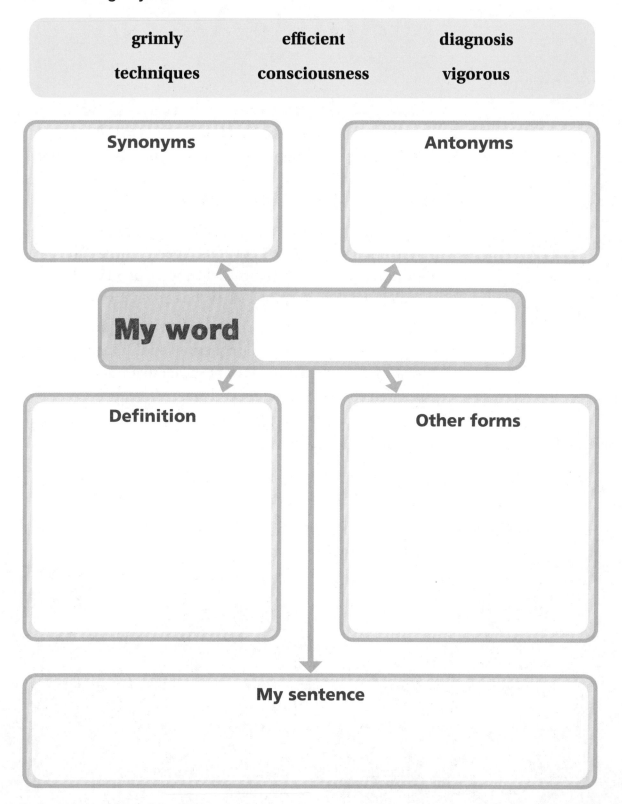

| grimly | efficient | diagnosis |
| techniques | consciousness | vigorous |

Synonyms

Antonyms

My word

Definition

Other forms

My sentence

Consider ▶ What might you discover if you could travel inside your body?

How are science fiction and fantasy similar? How are they different?

Muscle Voyage

POINT OF VIEW

You have read a story written in first-person point of view and one written in third-person point of view. Which point of view is used in this story? How can you tell?

1 The score was tied three to three, with five minutes left. It was not just any game. It was the last soccer game before Tanisha and her family moved from Florida to California. It was the last game before she had to say good-bye to all her friends at Dorchester Elementary. Her team, The Armadillos, had to win. Tanisha was determined to leave in glory.

Anything can happen in five minutes. Tanisha had played enough games to know that. She ran toward the ball and spotted an opening on the left. She made a few short dribbles and then a strong kick to the center. Score!

Tanisha raised her arms high in victory and jumped in the air. She heard her friends cheering loudly. Then suddenly Tanisha fell, clutching her lower leg. Her teammates and coach ran across the field toward her.

"What's wrong?" asked her friend Sheila. "You okay? You were great out there."

5 "My leg hurts really bad," said Tanisha, curled up on the grass. "I must have landed on it too hard or something."

"Better put some ice on that leg and have a doctor look at it right away," her coach urged.

Ten minutes later, Tanisha's father arrived. He punched the direction code to the health clinic into the dashboard of their automatic solar van. Within seconds they were zooming toward the clinic. In the waiting room, Tanisha held an ice pack against her leg, which still throbbed. The soccer game had been perfect, but now the day was ruined. The visit to the clinic would probably take forever, while her friends celebrated with pizza and a movie. Tanisha remembered the last moments of the game. *Anything can happen in five minutes.* That's for sure, she thought grimly.

A half hour passed slowly in the waiting room, then an hour. The plastic chairs seemed to grow harder.

"No wonder it's called a waiting room," Tanisha complained. "What if I'd cracked my head open? Would they keep us waiting this long?" A dozen hammers seemed to be at work on her calf muscle.

10   "Doctors have to see the sicker patients first," said her father. "And I've heard that the new imaging methods take longer."

"What kind of imaging methods?" Tanisha asked.

"You'll find out," said her father mysteriously.

Finally a young nurse led them into an examining room. A moment later the doctor arrived. She was tall and wore a white jumpsuit with the name *Dr. Juarez* in red on the pocket.

CONTEXT CLUES
Reread the first paragraph on this page. Circle the words in the text that help you understand what grimly means, and then write what you think grimly means on the lines below.

_____

_____

_____

MAKE INFERENCES
Paragraphs 9 and 10 show that Tanisha is feeling impatient. Circle the details that support this inference.

"Hello, young lady. What seems to be the matter with your leg?"

15   Tanisha explained how she had fallen on the field at the end of the soccer game.

"But my goal broke the tie!" she added.

"Congratulations! Soccer's a terrific sport," Dr. Juarez said. "I played it in school myself. But it's easy to get hurt, especially when you're tired at the end of a game. Let's get your leg feeling better fast." Dr. Juarez seemed both friendly and efficient.

Tanisha stretched her leg out on the examining table. Dr. Juarez poked and prodded. She spoke a few medical notes into a microphone on her wrist.

"Now it's time to take a closer look," said the doctor. "I believe you've strained your leg, Tanisha. To have a clear diagnosis, we need to know more about what's wrong. Our clinic is experimenting with some brand-new imaging techniques. With your permission, I'd like to take a quick journey inside your calf for a closer look."

20   "What do you mean by *inside* my calf?" said Tanisha, confused. "Like an X-ray?"

"Better than an X-ray," said Tanisha's father excitedly. "I've heard about these new techniques. Can you really go inside her leg, doctor?"

"Inside and back out again," said Dr. Juarez. "You've heard of the fifth level of consciousness, or awareness of reality?"

"Like gravity awareness?" Tanisha's father asked.

CONTEXT CLUES
Look at the surrounding sentences for clues that show what efficient means. Circle the clues. Then write a definition here.

_____

_____

_____

CHARACTER The story says Dr. Juarez seems friendly and efficient. Underline the details in the text that support this statement.

CHARACTER Based on what Tanisha's father says and the way he says it, what kind of person do you think he is?

_____

_____

_____

"Correct. Gravity awareness was the most important scientific breakthrough at the end of the twenty-first century. It made it possible for people to fly. Now scientists have mastered a sixth level. It is called the size, or shrinking level of consciousness. I will now demonstrate."

25 Dr. Juarez quickly slipped into a strange diving suit. She handed some earphones to Tanisha and her father. Then she pushed a button on the wall. There was a flash of light and a loud buzz. The air in the office crackled with electricity. Tanisha looked around, but Dr. Juarez was gone!

A moment later, Tanisha's earphones buzzed. "Tanisha? Can you hear me?"

"Dr. Juarez?" Tanisha asked. "Where are you?"

"I'm inside your leg, Tanisha. I'm swimming toward the calf muscle now." Dr. Juarez's voice sounded watery and far away.

"Swimming?" Tanisha gulped in amazement.

30 "Swimming," Dr. Juarez confirmed. "If you press the large red button on my computer, you'll see me on the monitor."

Tanisha pressed the button, and immediately an image of Dr. Juarez came on the screen. She was climbing onto something that looked like twisted ropes of taffy.

"I'm checking your calf muscle now," said Dr. Juarez. "Can you feel this?"

Tanisha felt a pinch. "Ouch!"

"The muscle is swollen and bruised," confirmed Dr. Juarez. "Looks like a bad strain. The good news is that it isn't torn."

SETTING This story is science fiction. It takes place during an imaginary future in which scientific discoveries have changed the way people live. What details in the setting show that the story is science fiction?

_____

_____

_____

MAKE INFERENCES Underline two details that show Dr. Juarez likes working with patients.

35

"What's that loud thumping sound?" asked Tanisha.

"That's your heart beating, Tanisha. It sounds strong and healthy. A strong heart is exactly what a good soccer player needs. Would you like to see what it looks like?"

"Sure!" said Tanisha. She couldn't believe that Dr. Juarez was really inside her body. Wait until her friends heard about this!

"I'll swim up toward your heart now," said Dr. Juarez.

Tanisha felt a tickle in her leg, as if a fly had crawled under her skin. A minute later the tickle was in her chest. The thumping sound grew louder than ever.

40

"Your heart is a muscle. It has four different sections, called chambers," explained Dr. Juarez, shouting to be heard. "I'm standing outside the right chamber now. This chamber pumps blood to your lungs. Can you see the veins on the muscle wall?"

"Yes! It's moving!" exclaimed Tanisha. With each thump, the muscle wall moved in and out.

"Your heart is about the size of your fist, Tanisha," Dr. Juarez explained. "It takes only about sixty seconds for your heart to pump blood to every cell in your body. Try squeezing and relaxing your fist. That's like the action of your heart."

THEME One theme of this story is that modern science can make life better. What is another theme of the story? Write a detail from the story that supports this theme.

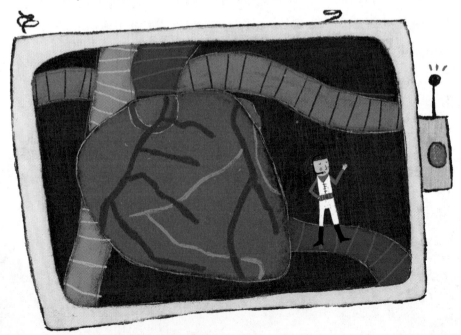

Tanisha tried it. She imagined blood pumping all the way from her heart to the sore muscle in her leg.

"Doesn't the heart get tired of pumping?" wondered Tanisha, thinking of how tired she had been at the end of the soccer game.

45 Dr. Juarez laughed. "Not a heart like yours," she said. "It's as healthy as an Amazon's. But if someone has an unhealthy heart, doctors can just swim inside the body and repair it. Back in the twenty-first century, heart surgery was difficult and dangerous. Today it's routine."

Dr. Juarez checked her watch. "I must leave the sixth level of consciousness now," she said. "See you in a minute."

Lights flashed, the air crackled, and suddenly Dr. Juarez was back in the office. She calmly stepped out of the diving suit and removed her headphones.

"Now let's talk face to face," she said. "That leg of yours is going to need to rest for a few weeks, Tanisha."

"A few weeks!" exclaimed Tanisha. "My family is moving to California next week. I'm going to a new school. How will I make friends if I can't play soccer?"

50 "I'm afraid that's your only choice," said Dr. Juarez firmly. "If you don't stay off that leg, the strain will get worse. Then it'll take even longer to heal."

For the past three months, Tanisha had talked about playing soccer in California. She had even been watching games online of the team at her new school. Her father knew how much soccer meant to her. He put his arm around Tanisha's shoulders.

"She'll rest the leg, Dr. Juarez," he said. "But is there anything we can do to prevent this from happening again?"

ALLUSION In Greek mythology, the Amazons were powerful female warriors. What does it mean that Tanisha's heart is as healthy as an Amazon's?

_____

_____

_____

MAKE INFERENCES Why do you think Dr. Juarez says that she must leave Tanisha's body? What clues did you use to make your inference?

_____

_____

_____

CONTEXT CLUES Based on context clues, what do you think vigorous means?

_____

_____

_____

PLOT The author uses dialogue to move the plot to a conclusion. Circle the dialogue that helps to end the story.

COMPARE THEMES "Muscle Voyage" and "A Monumental Mystery" are both about finding something. How are the themes of the two stories similar? How are they different?

_____

_____

_____

_____

"Yes," the doctor answered. "Always warm up well before your soccer games or any kind of vigorous exercise. Warm-ups take just a few minutes. Remember that important heart muscle we just looked at? The exercises are good for your heart, too."

Dr. Juarez showed Tanisha a chart of warm-up exercises. Her coach had shown the team a chart exactly like it. Tanisha hadn't thought the warm-ups helped much, so she had stopped doing them.

55   "Rest up, do those stretches, and you'll be playing soccer again soon, Tanisha," said Dr. Juarez. "This muscle strain won't stop you. And I'm sure you'll make lots of friends at your new school. Good-bye!"

And with that, Dr. Juarez disappeared. Tanisha and her father looked at each other in amazement.

"My friends won't believe this!" Tanisha cried. "Dr. Juarez went inside my body!"

"Let's see if they believe us," said her father. "Maybe that pizza party is still going on."

Off they zoomed in their solar van to find out.

Anchor Standard Discussion Questions

Discuss the following questions with your peer group. Then record your answers in the space provided.

1. Now that you have read "Secrets of the Sea," "A Monumental Mystery," and "Muscle Voyage," you are more familiar with first-person and third-person point of view. What are the advantages of telling a story from each point of view? Support your response using examples from at least two of the stories.

_____

_____

_____

_____

_____

2. Choose a sentence from "Secrets of the Sea," "A Monumental Mystery," or "Muscle Voyage" that you think needs more interesting and vivid language. Rewrite the sentence so that it contains figurative language. Then explain how your new version adds interest and fits the overall feeling of the story.

Original Sentence

Your Sentence

_____

_____

_____

Comprehension Check

1. What inferences can you make about Tanisha? What character traits does she reveal through her words and actions?

2. "Muscle Voyage" is told in the third person. In what ways would the story be different if it were told in the first person, from Dr. Juarez's point of view?

3. "Secrets of the Sea," "A Monumental Mystery," and "Muscle Voyage" all tell about amazing discoveries. Tell which discovery you think is the most interesting, and why. Use details from your reading to support your answer.

Read On Your Own

Read another short story, "A Helping Hoof," independently. Apply what you learned in this lesson and check your understanding.

Writing Fictional Narratives

Lesson 3

Drawing and painting are fun ways to be creative. In a drawing or a painting, you can invent people and worlds from your own imagination. You can even tell a story using nothing but illustrations. Now, think about creating people and worlds in writing. How can you turn the pictures in your head into language on paper? What might happen in a story you create? You can find out by writing a fictional narrative.

ESSENTIAL QUESTION

What makes a fictional narrative entertaining?

What's a Fictional Narrative?

Imagine a scene in your mind. It may be a scene in which someone is helping a friend. It may be a scene that features animals. It may even be a scene that takes place on another planet or deep under the earth. Any of these possible scenes could be the beginning of a fictional narrative.

In a **fictional narrative**, you tell a story that you make up yourself. Read the ways to make your fictional narrative entertaining.

Beginning
Introduce the characters and the setting.

Middle
Use narration to tell your story. Interesting details in the narration will create mental pictures for the reader. Strong dialogue will make your story convincing.

Ending
Bring your fictional narrative to a satisfying close.

Let's look at a fictional narrative.

Analyze a Mentor Text

This is an example of an entertaining fictional narrative by a fourth grader. Read it and then complete the activities in the boxes as a class.

A Hike with Cinnamon

"I promise I will help walk, feed, and take care of Cinnamon!" That was what Ian and his twin sister, Eve, both told their parents when they got a dog for their eleventh birthday. But that was two months ago, and Ian was exasperated. On days when it was his turn, Ian walked Cinnamon right after he got home from school. Even when he was tired, Ian was encouraged by Cinnamon's energy. The two of them were becoming good friends.

But Ian's sister Eve was another story. When she could have been walking the dog, she was often talking on the phone or e-mailing friends. Once she even told Ian she would pay him if he would walk Cinnamon for her. And a couple of times he had filled Cinnamon's empty dinner dish when it was Eve's turn to feed her. Ian had just about had it with his sister. He told her so, and she promised to do better. But she still forgot to do her part at times.

One weekend, their parents took the twins and Cinnamon on the dog's first excursion. They packed a picnic and set off on a hike through a state forest. Suddenly, they heard rustling in nearby trees, and a deer galloped away from them, its white tail flashing. Before any of them realized what was happening, Cinnamon bounded after the deer, jerking

BEGINNING The writer captures the reader's interest by revealing a promise the main characters made. This approach also introduces the characters to the reader. Draw a box around the main characters' names.

MIDDLE The writer uses interesting details to help the reader picture the narrative. Circle words that help the reader imagine the story.

MIDDLE The writer uses dialogue to make the narrative come to life. Underline the lines of dialogue.

ENDING Writers make sure the ending of the narrative is a conclusion that will satisfy readers. Draw a star by elements of the narrative that help make the ending satisfying.

her leash out of Eve's hand. What would they do now? The dog didn't know these woods. She would get lost!

Eve ran after the dog, ahead of the rest of her family. "Cinnamon! Come, Cinnamon!" she cried. They could see the dog running farther into the trees, but she paid no heed to Eve. "Cinnamon!" Eve screamed. Still the dog ran on.

Ian sprinted up to Eve. "Let me try." He called, "Come, Cinnamon! Come, girl!" and whistled loudly. They could no longer see or hear the dog. Ian's heart beat faster. "Here, girl! Come get a treat!" he called.

A moment passed. It seemed like the whole family was holding its breath. Then, suddenly, Cinnamon burst out of the trees and went right to Ian. He took hold of her leash and gave her a biscuit. They all praised Cinnamon for obeying him.

"I've learned something today," Eve said when all was quiet again. "I think Cinnamon likes Ian better than me. He has taken much better care of her, so she listens to him. For Cinnamon's safety, I need to care for her better." Cinnamon barked, as if to say she agreed. The whole family laughed.

Think About It ▶ What aspect of the narrative do you like best?

Do you find the narrative entertaining? Why or why not?

Vocabulary Study: Dictionary

A **dictionary** is a reference book that gives the meanings of words, as well as their parts of speech and pronunciations. When you find a word with a meaning you don't know, first try to define it using context clues. Then use a dictionary to confirm its meaning or, if context clues did not help you, to find the definition.

For example, read the sentence below. Use the context clues to define the word *heed*. Then use the dictionary entry below to confirm the word's meaning.

> They could see the dog running farther into the trees, but she paid no heed to Eve. "Cinnamon!" Eve screamed. Still the dog ran on.

heed (hēd**)** *n.* attention, notice

Look back at the fictional narrative on pages 47–48. Find each word that is written in the chart below. Look for context clues that help you figure out the word's meaning. Write these clues and the meaning you get from them in the chart. Then use a dictionary to check the word's meaning, and write the dictionary definition in the chart. Compare the meaning you got from the context with the dictionary meaning.

Word	Context Clues	Context Meaning	Dictionary Meaning
exasperated			
excursion			

Writing Process

Now that you have read and analyzed a fictional narrative, you are going to create your own by following these steps of the writing process.

1. Get Ready: Brainstorm Think about the main characters and events. Decide whether you want to write about things that could really happen or about make-believe things and places.

2. Organize Use a graphic organizer to plan your fictional narrative.

3. Draft Create the first draft of your fictional narrative.

4. Peer Review Work with a partner to evaluate and improve your draft.

5. Revise Use suggestions from your peer review to revise your fictional narrative.

6. Edit Check your work carefully for spelling, punctuation, and grammar errors.

7. Publish Create a final version of your fictional narrative.

Writing Assignment

In this lesson, you will write your own fictional narrative. As you create your narrative, remember the elements of the mentor text that were most interesting and effective. Read the following assignment.

Write a story about two friends who see a strange light in the sky. Suddenly, the light turns and starts to head in their direction. Your story should include three problems or conflicts the characters face before the strange light disappears.

Your story can be a wild, almost unbelievable tale, or it can be about events that could really happen. You are writing the story, so you get to decide!

1. Get Ready: Brainstorm

The first step in writing a fictional narrative is to choose your characters and setting. Begin by answering questions such as: Who are the main characters? Where and when does the story take place? Here's how the author of the mentor text brainstormed characters and setting.

Characters	Setting
Who Ian and Eve, twins; their dog, Cinnamon	**Where** at home and in a forest
Personality Ian: dedicated, faithful; Eve: somewhat lazy, means well	**When** in the present
	Details trees, brush, deer

Try It!   Use a Brainstorming Graphic Organizer

Now use the chart below to help brainstorm for details to include in your own fictional narrative about two friends who see a strange light in the sky.

Characters	Setting
Who _____	Where _____
Personality _____	When _____
	Details _____

Brainstorm Ideas for Your Narrative

Next, think of three problems your characters will face in the narrative. You can use a graphic organizer to think about how the events of the story develop because of the characters and setting. Here is how the author of the mentor text used the graphic organizer.

CHARACTERS Characters with strong traits will help you develop your story.

SETTING Deciding on the place and time of the narrative will help you create a believable world for your characters.

EVENTS The events in your story put the characters in situations where problems could happen.

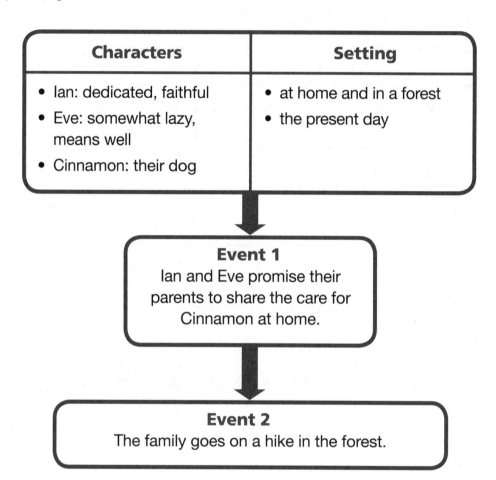

Characters	Setting
• Ian: dedicated, faithful • Eve: somewhat lazy, means well • Cinnamon: their dog	• at home and in a forest • the present day

Event 1
Ian and Eve promise their parents to share the care for Cinnamon at home.

Event 2
The family goes on a hike in the forest.

Try It!

Use a Graphic Organizer for Brainstorming

Now use the graphic organizer below to brainstorm how your characters and setting help develop the conflicts the characters face before the strange light disappears.

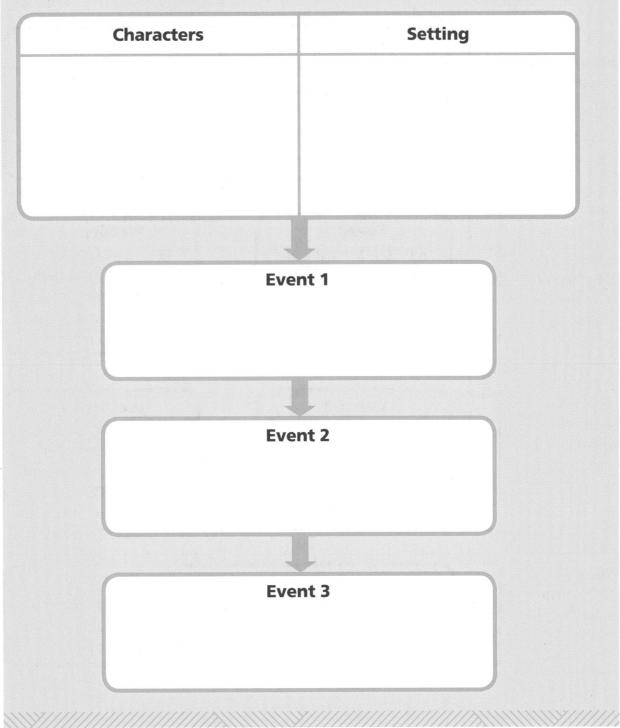

Characters	Setting

Event 1

Event 2

Event 3

2. Organize

You are almost ready to begin a draft of your fictional narrative. Create a story map by extending the graphic organizer on page 53 you used during brainstorming. Then add problems and a resolution. You can refer to this story map as you write your draft. The writer of the mentor text completed this story map.

BEGINNING Begin by introducing the characters and the setting.

Beginning

Characters	Setting
• Ian: dedicated, faithful • Eve: somewhat lazy, means well • Cinnamon: their dog	• at home • the present day

MIDDLE Think of how the events can develop naturally into problems. Remember to plan dialogue and exciting details to help you tell the events and problems.

Middle

Event 1
Ian and Eve promise their parents to share the care for Cinnamon at home.

→

Problem 1
Ian walks Cinnamon as soon as he gets home from school. Eve phones and e-mails friends instead.

Event 2
The family goes on a hike in the forest.

→

Problem 2
Cinnamon sees a deer and runs after it. Eve calls her over and over, but Cinnamon doesn't respond.

ENDING Think of an ending that will resolve the problems and satisfy the reader.

Ending

Resolution
Ian calls for Cinnamon. After a moment, Cinnamon comes back. Eve realizes she needs to do her part to care for the dog so that Cinnamon will respond to her, too.

Try It!

Organize Your Fictional Narrative

Now use the graphic organizer below to plan the narration and plot for your draft.

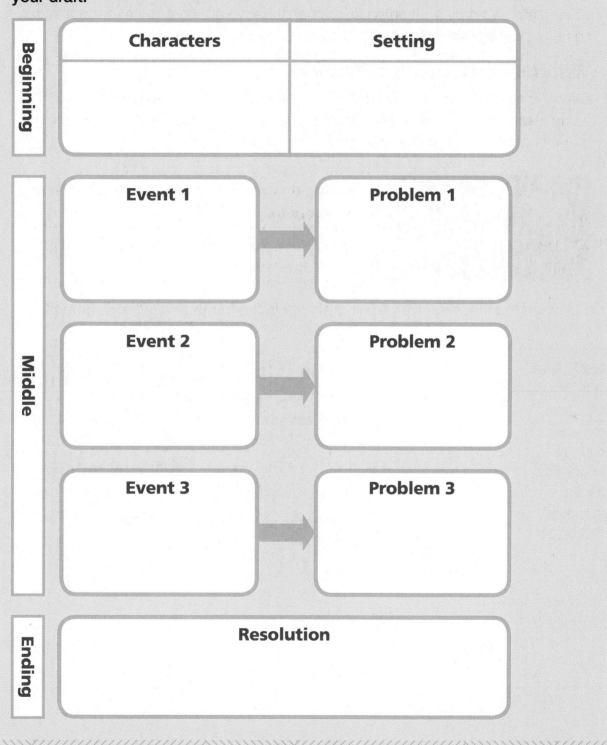

	Characters	Setting
Beginning		

Middle

Event 1 → Problem 1

Event 2 → Problem 2

Event 3 → Problem 3

Ending

Resolution

3. Draft

Now it is time to begin the first draft of your fictional narrative. Remember, your draft does not have to be perfect! This is the time to use your notes, get your story down in some sort of organized way, and have fun. You will have time to revise your writing later. Start by drafting your fictional narrative on a computer or on a separate sheet of paper. Make your characters and story come to life!

Writer's Craft: Using Dialogue

Dialogue makes your narrative more interesting and helps move the plot along. It can also reveal traits of your characters. Think about how the dialogue below might improve a narrative.

Moves the plot along	"Cleaning up the kitchen went so much faster with your help."
Reveals character traits	"I don't know, Sue. Are you sure we should go into that dark attic?"

The author of the mentor text uses dialogue in the fourth and fifth paragraphs.

DIALOGUE Read this section of the mentor text. Underline the lines of dialogue. Circle any dialogue that you think shows how Ian knows Cinnamon better than Eve.

Eve ran after the dog, ahead of the rest of her family. "Cinnamon! Come, Cinnamon!" she cried. They could see the dog running farther into the trees, but she paid no heed to Eve. "Cinnamon!" Eve screamed. Still the dog ran on.

Ian sprinted up to Eve. "Let me try." He called, "Come, Cinnamon! Come, girl!" and whistled loudly. They could no longer see or hear the dog. Ian's heart beat faster. "Here, girl! Come get a treat!" he called.

Try It! Write Your First Draft

On a computer or a separate sheet of paper, write the draft of your fictional narrative. Remember to use dialogue to move the plot along and to reveal character traits. Use this drafting checklist to help you as you write.

✓ A good beginning gets your reader's attention. You can begin with narration or with dialogue.

✓ Introduce the characters at the beginning of the narrative, and describe the setting.

✓ Develop the events and problems of the plot.

✓ Show how your characters deal with the problems in your story.

✓ Resolve the problems to end the story.

✓ Use dialogue to make the narrative interesting and to bring it to life.

Tips for Writing Your First Draft

- Write down key phrases and pieces of dialogue before you begin writing your draft. Sometimes this is a great warm-up to get you started!

- Think about what you would do if you were in your characters' shoes. This may help you figure out what happens next.

- Sometimes students think of good writing ideas while doing daily tasks. If you get stuck, try doing the dishes!

4. Peer Review

After you finish your draft, work with a partner to review each other's drafts. Here is a draft of the mentor text. Read it with your partner. Together, answer the questions in the boxes. Then we'll see how the writer's classmate evaluated the draft.

An Early Draft:

BEGINNING In the draft, the writer gives few details about the characters. What else might a reader want to know about the characters?

MIDDLE Dialogue gives characters a voice. What dialogue would you add?

ENDING The conclusion does not make clear why Eve thinks she needs to care for the dog better. What else might Eve say?

A Hike with Cinnamon

Ian and Eve got a dog for their eleventh birthday. They promised they would both take care of it. On days when it was his turn, Ian walked the dog right after school. But Eve wasn't always available to walk her.

One weekend, their parents took the twins on a hike through a state forest. Suddenly, they saw a deer gallop away. Before any of them realized what was happening, Cinnamon followed the deer.

Eve ran after the dog, ahead of the rest of her family. She called Cinnamon. They could see the dog running farther into the trees, but she paid no heed to Eve. Eve called louder. Still the dog ran on.

Ian sprinted up to Eve. "Let me try." He called, "Come, Cinnamon! Come, girl!" and whistled loudly. They could no longer see or hear the dog. "Here, girl! Come get a treat!" Ian called. Suddenly, Cinnamon burst out of the trees and went right to Ian. They all praised Cinnamon for obeying him.

"I've learned something today," Eve said when all was quiet again. "I need to care for Cinnamon better." Cinnamon barked, as if to say she agreed. The whole family laughed.

An Example Peer Review Form

This peer review form gives an example of how a classmate evaluated the draft of the mentor text shown on page 58.

The narrative includes a strong beginning, middle, and ending. **The beginning introduces the characters and setting.**	You did a good job of introducing the dog at the beginning. You could improve your fictional narrative by telling how Ian cares for his dog and by giving examples of how Eve does not care for the dog.
The plot develops from the events that happen and the problems the characters face. **The writer shows how the characters deal with the problems.**	You did a good job of showing that the hike in the forest is important to the narrative. You could improve your fictional narrative by making it clearer that Cinnamon is the dog and she went on the hike with the family.
The writer uses dialogue to move the plot along, to show the characters' traits, and to make the narrative interesting.	You did a good job of using dialogue to show how Ian called Cinnamon. You could improve your fictional narrative by adding dialogue in which Eve calls Cinnamon.
The ending shows how the problems are resolved. **The writer makes the ending satisfying to the reader.**	You did a good job of wrapping up the narrative in the last two sentences. You could improve your fictional narrative by making it clearer why Eve thinks she needs to care for Cinnamon better.

Try It!

Peer Review with a Partner

Now you are going to work with a partner to review each other's fictional narrative drafts. You will use the peer review form below. If you need help, look back at the mentor text writer's peer review form for suggestions.

The narrative includes a strong beginning, middle, and ending. **The beginning introduces the characters and setting.**	You did a good job of You could improve your fictional narrative by
The plot develops from the events that happen and the problems the characters face. **The writer shows how the characters deal with the problems.**	You did a good job of You could improve your fictional narrative by
The writer uses dialogue to move the plot along, to show the characters' traits, and to make the narrative interesting.	You did a good job of You could improve your fictional narrative by
The ending shows how the problems are resolved. **The writer makes the ending satisfying to the reader.**	You did a good job of You could improve your fictional narrative by

Try It!   Record Key Peer Review Comments

Now it's time for you and your partner to share your comments with each other. Listen to your partner's feedback, and write down the key comments in the left column. Then write some ideas for improving your draft in the right column.

My review says the beginning	I will
My review says that the characters	I will
My review says that the setting	I will
My review says that the problems	I will
My review says that the dialogue	I will
My review says that the ending	I will

Use the space below to write anything additional you notice about your draft that you think you can improve.

5. Revise

In this step of the writing process, you work on parts of your draft that need improvement. Use the peer review form that your classmate completed to help you. You also use your own ideas about how to improve each part of your fictional narrative. This checklist includes some things to think about as you get ready to revise.

Revision Checklist

✔ Does my beginning introduce the characters and setting well?

✔ Do the events develop naturally from the characters and setting?

✔ Does the middle introduce problems and show how the characters deal with them?

✔ Does the ending resolve the problems? Is it a satisfying ending?

✔ Do I use dialogue to move the plot along, reveal the characters' traits, and make the narrative interesting?

✔ Do I use sensory language to make my narrative come to life?

Writer's Craft: Using Sensory Language

Using words that appeal to the five senses makes your fictional narrative lively and more convincing. For example, instead of writing *The rain fell on the roof,* you might write, *The rain pounded on the hot roof.* Instead of writing *The flower opened,* you might write, *The pink flower burst open.* Now look at the mentor text for examples of sensory language.

SENSORY LANGUAGE
Sensory language appeals to the senses of hearing, sight, smell, taste, and touch. Underline sensory language in this paragraph.

One weekend, their parents took the twins and Cinnamon on the dog's first excursion. They packed a picnic and set off on a hike through a state forest. Suddenly, they heard rustling in nearby trees, and a deer galloped away from them, its white tail flashing. Before any of them realized what was happening, Cinnamon bounded after the deer, jerking her leash out of Eve's hand. What would they do now? The dog didn't know these woods. She would get lost!

Try It!

Revise Your Fictional Narrative

Replacing simple words with sensory words is an important part of revising. Practice using sensory language with the following paragraph. Replace each underlined word with a sensory word. Write your answers on the lines below the paragraph.

> Camping in the mountains is fun. I love hearing the <u>sound</u> of hamburgers cooking over the fire. The rising sun <u>appears</u> above the lake each morning. My boots <u>step</u> solidly on the rocks that I climb by the lake.

Replace *sound* with _____

Replace *appears* with _____

Replace *step* with _____

Writing Assignment

Now it's time to revise the draft of your fictional narrative. Continue working on a computer or on a separate sheet of paper. Review the assignment, repeated below, and the revision checklist. Doing so will help you know that you have included everything you need.

> Write a story about two friends who see a strange light in the sky. Suddenly, the light turns and starts to head in their direction. Your story should include three problems or conflicts the characters face before the strange light disappears.
>
> Your story can be a wild, almost unbelievable tale, or it can be about events that could really happen. You are writing the story, so you get to decide!

6. Edit

After revising your fictional narrative, you will edit it. When you edit, you read very carefully to be sure to find any mistakes in your writing. Here's a checklist of some things to look for as you edit.

Editing Checklist

✔ Did you indent each paragraph?

✔ Are all of your sentences complete? Does each have a subject and a verb?

✔ Did you begin each sentence with a capital letter?

✔ Does each sentence end with the correct punctuation?

✔ Have you used commas correctly?

✔ Are all of your words spelled correctly?

If you typed your narrative, print it out so you can mark it up. You can use these editing marks to mark any errors you find.

⌐ Indent   ⌃ Add   ⊙ Period   Ⅵ Insert quotation marks

This is a paragraph from the draft of the mentor text showing how to use editing marks.

⌐I've learned something today, Eve said when all was quiet

again, "I need to care for Cinnamon better." Cinnamon

as
barked, if to say she agreed. The whole family laughed.
  ⌃

Language Focus

Complete Sentences

A complete sentence includes a subject and a predicate. A subject is what or whom the sentence is about. The predicate tells what the subject does and contains the verb. Note the subject and predicate in the sentence below.

Subject	Predicate
Milo and his little sister	ran to school.

A **complete sentence** begins with a capital letter and ends with a period, a question mark, or an exclamation point. A **fragment** is a series of words missing either a subject or a predicate. A **run-on** is one or more sentences run together without proper end punctuation. See the examples in the chart below.

> **Run-on:** This salad tastes good, it has carrots in it.
>
> **Correction:** This salad tastes good! It has carrots in it.
>
> **Fragment:** The sunlight on my face.
>
> **Correction:** The sunlight is on my face.

Capitalization

Every sentence begins with a capital letter. Capital letters are also used for proper nouns and proper adjectives, and for the first word of dialogue and titles.

Frequently Confused Words

Many words are often confused with other words that sound the same. Make sure each word is the correct one for its context.

Examples: to, too, two; their, they're; it's, its

Ian sprinted up to Eve. "Let me try." He called, "Come, Cinnamon! Come, girl!" and whistled loudly. They could no longer see or hear the dog. Ian's heart beat faster. "Here, girl! Come get a treat!" he called.

COMPLETE SENTENCES
Read this section of the mentor text. Underline the last complete sentence in the paragraph.

Try It!   Language and Editing Practice

Underline the words in each sentence that should be capitalized.

1. You can see that i am not ready to go to the zoo.

2. Wanda watched michael walk up the steps of the lincoln memorial.

3. In august we will go to the gulf of mexico for our vacation.

4. My grandparents took a cruise last year down the nile river.

5. The jet plane flew over death valley, utah, and denver, colorado.

Now use editing marks to correct the sentence fragments, run-on sentences, and incorrect words in this paragraph.

My school lunch always includes a sandwich. Carrots and milk. Often

their is a cookie, to. My favorite part, though, is the vegetable chips my

mom buys from the health food store, they are delicious. I like to eat my

lunch and than spend time with my friends.

Try It!   Edit Your Fictional Narrative

Now edit your fictional narrative. Use this checklist and the editing marks you have learned to correct any errors you find.

- [ ] Did you indent each paragraph?

- [ ] Are all of your sentences complete? Have you corrected fragments and run-ons?

- [ ] Did you begin each sentence with a capital letter? Did you capitalize proper nouns and adjectives?

- [ ] Does each sentence end with the correct punctuation mark?

- [ ] Have you used commas correctly?

- [ ] Are all of your words spelled correctly?

- [ ] Have you used frequently confused words correctly?

Editing Tips

- Read your writing aloud. This will help you discover missing words and awkward phrases. Ask yourself, "Did that sound right?"

- Listen carefully as you read for stops and pauses. Stops and pauses usually indicate the places where punctuation might go. Ask yourself, "Am I missing any punctuation?"

- Read backward from the end of your writing, one sentence at a time. This may help you catch mistakes you would not notice otherwise.

7. Publish

On a computer or a separate sheet of paper, create a neat final draft of your fictional narrative. Correct all errors that you identified while editing your draft. Be sure to give your fictional narrative an interesting title.

The final step is to publish your fictional narrative. Here are some different ways you might choose to share your work.

- Create a class anthology that collects your and your classmates' fictional narratives.

- With a small group of your classmates, read your fictional narrative aloud as a dramatic presentation.

- Get permission to read your fictional narrative aloud to students from another class.

- Illustrate your fictional narrative with pictures of characters or events.

- Bind your fictional narrative with staples or spiral binding, or place it in a folder.

Technology Suggestions
- **Upload your fictional narrative onto your class or school blog.**
- **Scan illustrations for your fictional narrative, and create a printed booklet.**

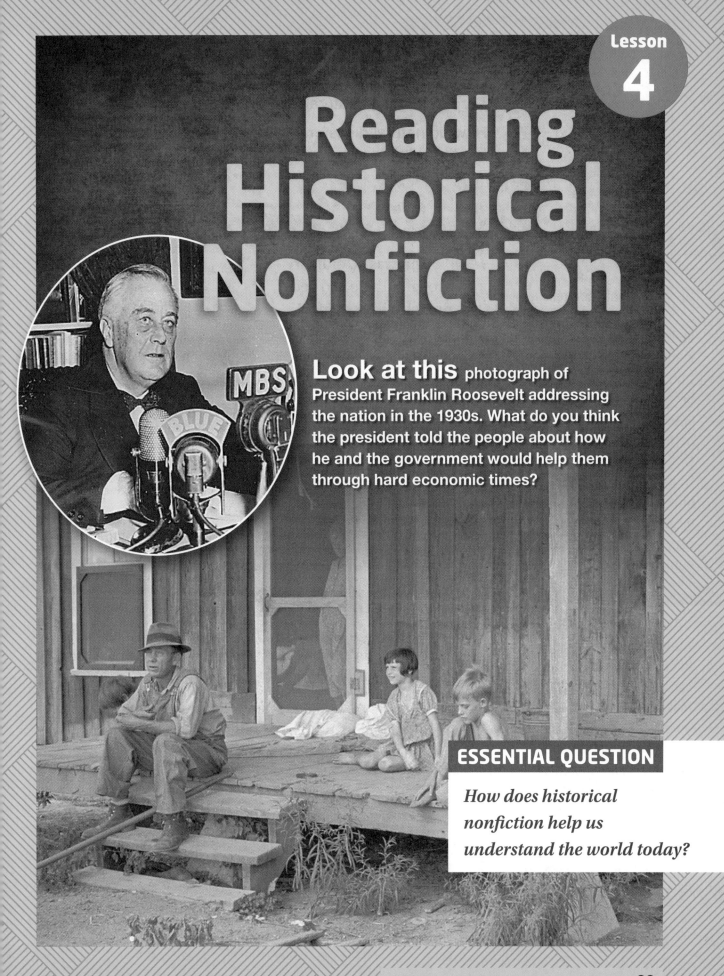

Reading Historical Nonfiction

Look at this photograph of President Franklin Roosevelt addressing the nation in the 1930s. What do you think the president told the people about how he and the government would help them through hard economic times?

ESSENTIAL QUESTION

How does historical nonfiction help us understand the world today?

Consider ▶ What can we learn from firsthand and secondhand accounts of past natural disasters?

How do natural disasters affect the lives of people who live through them?

This Time Was Different

HISTORICAL NONFICTION

Historical nonfiction tells about real events or people in the past. All of the details in historical nonfiction are true. These accounts may be written by firsthand witnesses, people who participated in the events. Or they may be written by people who did not directly participate in the events. What challenges do people face in this historical nonfiction account?

CAUSE AND EFFECT

Authors sometimes organize information by describing causes and effects. A cause makes something occur, and an effect is the result of the cause. Paragraphs 2 and 3 have a cause and effect structure. In paragraph 2, the cause is "enough rain falls." What are the effects of this cause? What are the causes and effects in paragraph 3?

1   This was no ordinary drought. There had been droughts before, and there would be others in the future. But this time was different. This was the worst drought in U.S. history. Many farms and other businesses failed. Millions of people fled their homes on the Southern Plains during the severe drought, which lasted for nearly ten years.

A serious drought poses dangers for people and wildlife. Areas hit by such a drought often need years to recover from its effects.

In normal times, enough rain falls to keep lakes and rivers at their usual levels. Lakes and streams are full of life. Deer and other animals drink the water. Bears may come to look for fish. People use the water for recreation, such as swimming or fishing. When there is normal rainfall, farmers use water from these reservoirs to grow their crops. They also use it to provide water for their animals.

Sometimes, however, there is not enough rainfall. When this happens, there is less water in the rivers and streams. Without enough water, some animals cannot survive. Crops may not grow well, or they may not grow at all. Without water, the soil dries up and easily blows away. During these dry spells, it is also often very hot. The heat causes the water left in lakes and rivers to evaporate, or dry up. The effects of a serious drought can last for years.

For many years in the early 1900s, agriculture, or farming, thrived on the Southern Plains. The soil was fertile, and crops grew well. Farmers expected their good fortune to continue. But in 1931, the rains stopped. Farmers in Texas, Oklahoma, Kansas, and other states saw their crops wither and their harvests shrink. Without crops to sell, many could not afford to keep their farms running. Because farmers had no money to spend, other local businesses and banks began to suffer as a result. People across the region longed for rain, but the drought continued for several years.

5   During this time, dust storms came often. Strong winds blew dirt, dust, and soil in large clouds across hundreds of miles. Fertile topsoil, so important for raising crops, was quickly blown away. Anyone outdoors could easily get lost. It was often hard to breathe or to see even a few feet ahead. Dirt from the dust storms piled up against barns and houses. It surrounded cars and farm machines. It got into the engines and ruined them. It swallowed up crops, leaving little to harvest. Livestock that breathed in the dust often got sick and died. The dust even got into people's houses. It coated anything that was not covered. Because these storms brought dark clouds of dirt and dust, they became known as "black blizzards."

ROOTS AND AFFIXES
The word *culture* comes from a Latin word meaning "to grow." The prefix *agri-* comes from the Greek word for field or soil. Together, they give us the word *agriculture*, which means "the science or occupation of farming." What other words do you know that end with the root *culture*? What do you think *aquaculture* means?

MAIN IDEA The main idea of a passage is what the passage is mostly about. Details are ideas, information, or examples that support the main idea. In paragraph 5, the main idea is that the dust storms were dangerous and destructive. One supporting detail is that "it was often hard to breathe or to see even a few feet ahead." What other supporting details show that the dust storms were dangerous and destructive events?

Nebraska

Colorado

Kansas

New Mexico

Oklahoma

Texas

Areas with the most extreme drought

Millions of acres across several states were affected by years of drought in the 1930s.

Rather than rain, storms during the Dust Bowl brought enormous clouds of dust and dirt that covered everything in their path.

Black Sunday

The brutal dust storms lasted for weeks. But on the morning of Sunday, April 14, 1935, the weather actually seemed pleasant. The dust storms had stopped, and the sun began to shine for the first time in months. Many people hoped to catch up on outdoor activities, such as hanging out their laundry or just playing outside.

The break from dust storms did not last long. In the afternoon, the temperature began to fall. Soon dark clouds blocked the sun. The sky turned black, and a choking dust storm struck. The churning cloud may have been more than a mile tall. People raced to get indoors. Strangers took shelter with one another. Because drivers could not see the road ahead of them, cars and trucks were forced to stop in the middle of the street. It seemed that nothing could stop the dust from getting into people's houses. Soon everything was covered by the dust. It easily blew through the cracks in the walls and onto dishes, food, and clothes. When the dust storm was over, people had to shovel out what was left of their lives. It took people months to add up the cost of the damage. After the Black Sunday storm, reporters began to refer to the Southern Plains region as the "Dust Bowl." The name stuck, and today we remember that decade of drought as the Dust Bowl era.

Could It Happen Again?

The Dust Bowl lasted until 1939 and changed millions of people's lives. Many headed west to California to escape the drought and seek a better life. The government of the United States tried to help those who stayed in the Southern Plains. They taught people ways to protect the soil from erosion. Erosion occurs when soil is loose enough for the wind to blow it away. Erosion often occurs when there are no plant roots to hold the soil in place. The Southern Plains region had once been grassland. The grass held the soil in place and kept it from blowing away. Farmers, however, had planted wheat. This crop did not protect the soil as well as the grass had. More and more cattle were also grazing, and this meant that even more grassland was lost. Then the drought hit, making the dry soil even more dry and easier to blow away. Scientists who understood good farming methods shared what they knew. For example, they said that planting lines of trees alongside fields would break the force of the wind. Scientists also predicted that if farmers followed good soil and water conservation methods, there would never again be another Dust Bowl.

Were they right? There have always been droughts. There are places in the United States that are going through droughts right now. Still, scientists say that if people follow good soil and water conservation methods, there should be no more Dust Bowl eras.

CAUSE AND EFFECT
Historical nonfiction helps us to understand what caused things to happen in the past. It also teaches us the effects of events such as natural disasters and what we might expect the next time something like this happens. Was the drought the only cause of the Dust Bowl? According to the account, what else helped to cause the Dust Bowl?

To prevent wind erosion, farmers often plant rows of trees alongside their fields.

Consider ▶ In what ways is historical nonfiction especially valuable when it is told by firsthand witnesses or by participants in an event?

Do accounts told by people who took part in an event always give us the clearest picture of that event?

FIRSTHAND ACCOUNT President Roosevelt says, "I have been on a journey," and describes what he saw. That means that this text is a firsthand account by someone who participated in the historical events described. How does that make this account different from "This Time Was Different"?

MAIN IDEA The main idea of this section is that the president saw great hardship in the areas he visited. What details or facts support the main idea?

President Roosevelt's Fireside Chat

1   *During the hard economic times of the 1930s, President Franklin D. Roosevelt often spoke to the nation through informal radio addresses, known as "fireside chats." The following is part of his fireside chat given in September of 1936, in the middle of the Dust Bowl era.*

I have been on a journey. . . . I went primarily to see at first hand conditions in the drought states; to see how effectively Federal and local authorities are taking care of pressing problems of relief and also how they are to work together to defend the people of this country against the effects of future droughts.

I saw drought devastation in nine states.

I talked with families who had lost their wheat crop, lost their corn crop, lost their livestock, lost the water in their well, lost their garden and come through to the end of the summer without one dollar of cash resources, facing a winter without feed or food—facing a planting season without seed to put in the ground.

5   That was the extreme case, but there are thousands and thousands of families on western farms who share the same difficulties.

President Roosevelt often gave fireside chats to help people understand the problems that the country faced in the 1930s.

I saw cattlemen who because of lack of grass or lack of winter feed have been compelled to sell all but their breeding stock and will need help to carry even these through the coming winter. I saw livestock kept alive only because water had been brought to them long distances in tank cars. I saw other farm families who have not lost everything but who, because they have made only partial crops, must have some form of help if they are to continue farming next spring.

I shall never forget the fields of wheat so blasted by heat that they cannot be harvested. I shall never forget field after field of corn stunted, earless, and stripped of leaves, for what the sun left, the grasshoppers took. I saw brown pastures which would not keep a cow on fifty acres.

Yet I would not have you think for a single minute that there is permanent disaster in these drought regions, or that the picture I saw meant depopulating these areas. No cracked earth, no blistering sun, no burning wind, no grasshoppers, are a permanent match for the indomitable[1] American farmers and stockmen and their wives and children who have carried on through desperate days, and inspire us with their self-reliance, their tenacity, and their courage. It was their fathers' task to make homes; it is their task to keep those homes; it is our task to help them with their fight. . . .

Beginning in 1934, when we also had serious drought conditions, the state and Federal governments cooperated in planning a large number of projects—many of them directly aimed at the alleviation of future drought conditions. In accordance with that program, literally thousands of ponds or small reservoirs have been built in order to supply water for stock and to lift the level of the underground water to protect wells from going dry. Thousands of wells have been drilled or deepened; community lakes have been created, and irrigation projects are being pushed.

[1] **indomitable** not easily defeated

ROOTS AND AFFIXES
Look at the word *earless* in paragraph 7. What does the root word *ear* mean in this context? The suffix *-less* means "without." Use this clue to tell what the word *earless* means.

MAKE INFERENCES
Not all information needs to be directly stated. Authors expect readers to use prior knowledge to connect details and make inferences. In his fireside chat, Roosevelt speaks about the self-reliance and courage of American farmers and their families. What can you infer was his reason for saying this?

President Roosevelt traveled from state to state and met with farmers struggling through the drought.

MAKE INFERENCES
President Roosevelt's audience included people who agreed with him and people who disagreed with him. He says, "Spending like this is not waste." What inference can you draw from this detail about the views of listeners who disagreed with the president?

COMPARE AND CONTRAST To compare and contrast means to note similarities and differences in people, places, or events. In paragraph 12, President Roosevelt compares and contrasts what will happen if the government helps farmers and what will happen if it doesn't help them. According to the passage, what will happen to the farmers if they do not get government help?

10   Water conservation by means such as these is being expanded as a result of this new drought all through the Great Plains area, the western corn belt and in the states that lie further south. . . .

Spending like this is not waste. It would spell future waste if we did not spend for such things now. These emergency work projects provide money to buy food and clothing for the winter; they keep the livestock on the farm; they provide seed for a new crop; and, best of all, they will conserve soil and water in the future in those areas most frequently hit by drought.

If, for example, in some local area the water table continues to drop and the topsoil to blow away, the land values will disappear with the water and the soil. People on the farms will drift into the nearby cities; the cities will have no farm trade and the workers in the city factories and stores will have no jobs. Property values in the cities will decline. If, on the other hand, the farms within that area remain as farms with better water supply and no erosion, the farm population will stay on the land and prosper, and the nearby cities will prosper, too. Property values will increase instead of disappearing. That is why it is worth our while as a nation to spend money in order to save money. . . .

As the hard times continued, many people could not afford to keep their homes or farms. Millions of people had to leave the Southern Plains and search for work elsewhere.

Americans worked together to bring farms back to life after years of drought and dust storms. They hoped their efforts would keep the Dust Bowl era from ever occurring again.

The people in the drought area do not want to be dependent on Federal, state or any other kind of charity. They want for themselves and their families an opportunity to share fairly by their own efforts in the progress of America. . . .

In the drought area people are not afraid to use new methods to meet changes in Nature, and to correct mistakes of the past. If overgrazing has injured range lands, they are willing to reduce the grazing. If certain wheat lands should be returned to pasture, they are willing to cooperate. If trees should be planted as windbreaks or to stop erosion, they will work with us. If terracing or summer fallowing[2] or crop rotation is called for, they will carry them out. They stand ready to fit, and not to fight, the ways of Nature.

15 We are helping, and shall continue to help the farmer to do those things, through local soil conservation committees and other cooperative local, state and Federal agencies of government. . . .

With this fine help, we are tiding over the present emergency. We are going to conserve soil, conserve water and conserve life. We are going to have long-time defenses against both low prices and drought. We are going to have a farm policy that will serve the national welfare. That is our hope for the future.

> **MAIN IDEA** The first and last sentences of a paragraph can help you find its main idea. What is the main idea of paragraph 14? What details support the main idea?

[2] **fallowing** plowing land without seeding it

Comprehension Check

Look back at "This Time Was Different" and "President Roosevelt's Fireside Chat." What did people learn from the Dust Bowl? What steps did they take to prevent such a devastating drought from happening again? How did each of these steps help? Use this information to complete the chart below.

Steps	How the Steps Helped
1. Farmers planted lines of trees next to their fields.	The trees helped block the wind and prevent erosion.
2. Government programs helped build reservoirs.	
3.	
4.	

Vocabulary

Use the word map below to help you define and use one of the highlighted vocabulary words from the Share and Learn reading or another word your teacher assigns you.

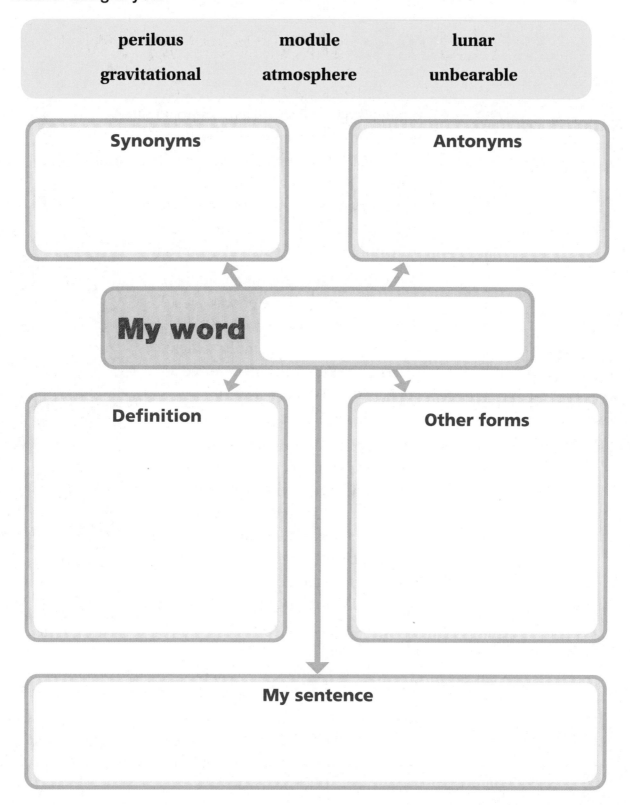

perilous   module   lunar

gravitational   atmosphere   unbearable

Synonyms

Antonyms

My word

Definition

Other forms

My sentence

Consider ▶ What does this article have in common with the earlier passages?

In what ways is Commander Jim Lovell's outlook similar to President Roosevelt's outlook?

Jim Lovell: Stranded in Space

HISTORICAL NONFICTION Is this passage a firsthand or secondhand account? How can you tell?

_____

_____

_____

ASK AND ANSWER QUESTIONS What question can you ask and answer about this section to make sure you understand its main idea?

_____

_____

_____

1   3 . . . 2 . . . 1 . . . Blast off! A young teenager named Jim Lovell set off a rocket that bolted 80 feet into the air, staggered, exploded—and then crashed. The launch of Lovell's first rocket, which he had built with help from his friends and chemistry teacher, was a breathtaking and beautiful failure. But that didn't stop him from hoping to fly a real rocket one day.

Lovell pursued his dream at the U.S. Naval Academy, where he was a test pilot. One of his jobs was to land his jet on an aircraft carrier runway at night. It was a **perilous** task that required a cool head and nerves of steel.

In 1962, NASA selected the young test pilot for its astronaut program. Lovell was going to do what he had always dreamed of doing—fly rockets. Lovell spent hundreds of hours in space on two of the early Gemini missions in the mid-1960s. Then, in 1968, he was a pilot and navigator on the Apollo 8 mission. For the first time ever, humans left Earth's orbit and journeyed to the moon. However, the Apollo 8 mission was to enter the moon's orbit, not to land on the moon's surface. As Neil Armstrong's backup, Lovell would have to watch on television as astronauts from the Apollo 11 mission walked on the moon in 1969. Lovell hoped that he would walk on the moon on his next mission, Apollo 13.

Courtesy of NASA

Jim Lovell and the crew of the *Odyssey* took off and headed for the moon on April 11, 1970.

"Houston, We've Had a Problem Here"

On April 11, 1970, Lovell sat down behind the controls as the commander of the *Odyssey* alongside his crew, Jack Swigert and Fred Haise. The three men began their ten-day mission to the moon. They traveled more than 200,000 miles in just 56 hours. The mission had gone smoothly up to that point. It had even included a live TV broadcast for people back on Earth.

5   Knowing they had nearly reached their destination, the crew prepared for landing on the moon. Suddenly they heard a loud bang, and the spacecraft shuddered. A high-pitched alarm sounded in the command module. Warning lights flashed on the spacecraft's control panels. The dials said there was not enough battery power to run the lights, heat, and electronic equipment. Lovell knew they were in trouble; he just didn't know how much.

Back at Mission Control, in Houston, Texas, NASA officials heard Jack Swigert's voice crackle over the radio—"Houston, we've had a problem here." The now-historic message vastly understated the seriousness of the situation. Looking out the window, Lovell and his crew saw a cloud of white gas. It was leaking out of the spacecraft and floating into space. An oxygen tank had exploded, leaving a gaping hole in the side of the service module. *Odyssey* was quickly losing oxygen, water, and electrical power. Soon the astronauts would not be able to operate the spacecraft. They wouldn't be able to land on the moon as they had planned.

After the accident, the Apollo 13 crew had to figure out how to travel more than 200,000 miles to get back to Earth.

CAUSE AND EFFECT
Find the place on this page that describes the cause of the problems on the *Odyssey*. Circle this sentence. Then find the descriptions of the effects that this event caused. Underline these effects.

COMPARE AND CONTRAST Compare how Lovell and his crew most likely feel in paragraph 4 with how they feel in paragraph 6.

_____

_____

_____

MAKE CONNECTIONS
Reread paragraph 7. What is the problem that the astronauts and Mission Control need to solve?

_____

_____

_____

Now look at paragraphs 8 and 9. Underline two key words that give you clues about how the information is organized. Then write what these words tell you about how the astronauts and Mission Control will solve their problem.

_____

_____

_____

Mission Control in High Gear

Fortunately, Lovell and his crew were not completely alone. Hundreds of scientists, engineers, and mathematicians at Mission Control shifted into high gear. How much fuel was left? Was there enough oxygen? How would they turn the command module around and get it back to Earth? The teams at Mission Control would have to work around the clock to solve these problems if they were going to help the astronauts get home alive.

First, they needed to figure out how to make the oxygen and battery power last as long as possible. If the astronauts stayed in the command module, they would be out of air in a few hours. The crew had to move to the lunar module right away. The lunar module was a small, separate section of the spacecraft that would have been used to land on the moon. It was connected to one end of the command module, and it had extra batteries and oxygen. This would buy the crew some time. But the lunar module had been built to last only forty-five hours and to support only two people. Could it last for the ninety or more hours it would take to get the three astronauts back to Earth?

The next problem was how to turn the ship around. Mission Control and the astronauts decided to blast the ship's rockets at just the right moment to make it swing around the moon. They would use the gravitational pull of the moon to direct the spacecraft back toward Earth.

Teams of experts at Mission Control worked day and night to bring the Apollo 13 crew home safely.

A Risky Return

10   Although they were finally headed in the right direction, the astronauts were running out of water. The lunar module's batteries did not have enough power to last, so Lovell and his crew had to turn off nearly every electrical device. The temperature on the ship dropped to near freezing. The windows started frosting up. Back at Mission Control in Houston, however, everyone was drenched in sweat. Quickly they figured out new instructions for Lovell's crew to use to operate the damaged ship. It took the astronauts hours to carefully copy down the detailed instructions. A single error could have made the difference between life and death.

The lunar module could work as a lifeboat to get the astronauts back toward Earth. But it didn't have the heat shield needed to make it through Earth's atmosphere. For this part of the trip, the crew would need to use the command module, which had gone without power for days. Its batteries were weak. The module's walls were covered with tiny drops of water. The crew worried that the dampness and cold might have damaged the electronic equipment. Step by step, the team at Mission Control worked with the astronauts to power up the command module. This was something that had never before been done in the middle of a mission.

Now came the most dangerous part of the mission. Strapped in their seats, Lovell, Swigert, and Haise hurtled toward home. Even if they followed the instructions perfectly, nobody knew whether the fragile ship would survive the fiery reentry into Earth's atmosphere.

Despite its limited power, the lunar module allowed the crew to survive the long trip back from the moon.

Courtesy of NASA

MAKE INFERENCES
In paragraph 10, the author says the people at Mission Control were "drenched in sweat." What inference can you make about the people at Mission Control based on this detail?

_____

_____

_____

CAUSE AND EFFECT
What caused the temperature on the ship to drop to near freezing? Circle the sentence that tells the cause.

MAIN IDEA In paragraph 11, the main idea is that the command module might not work to bring the astronauts back to Earth. Underline two details that support this main idea.

ROOTS AND AFFIXES
The prefix *un-* means
"not." The suffix *-able*
means "capable of." Use
these clues to write a
definition for unbearable.

_____

_____

_____

MAKE INFERENCES
Could the crew of the
Apollo 13 mission
have made it home
without the help of
Mission Control? Why
or why not?

_____

_____

_____

MAIN IDEA Underline
two details that support
the main idea that the
astronauts were
honored even though
their mission failed.

At Mission Control in Houston, four unbearable minutes passed as the ship entered the atmosphere. No sound came from the astronauts because the intense heat around the spacecraft prevented radio communication. Would the heat shield still work? Would the ship's parachutes open? There was nothing anyone could do but wait and see. At last, Lovell's voice came over the speakers in Houston. He said one word: "Okay." Cheers erupted at Mission Control. Soon, the parachutes opened on the command module, and the Apollo 13 crew landed gently in the South Pacific Ocean. Within an hour, they were safely on board the USS *Iwo Jima* recovery ship.

The Apollo 13 crew members were brought back to Hawaii, where they found their families waiting for them. President Richard Nixon arrived and awarded the crew members the Presidential Medal of Freedom—the highest honor that can be given to an American civilian. It was only when he was in Hawaii that Lovell realized how carefully watched their trip had been. Millions of people in countries around the world had intently followed the story on television, on the radio, and in newspapers.

15   NASA declared the Apollo 13 mission a "successful failure." The crew never landed on the moon, but they avoided a tragedy. Quick thinking, teamwork, and bravery had helped bring the astronauts safely back home. Later, Commander Jim Lovell would say, "I never got to the point where I didn't have enough hope to keep going."

After safely returning to Earth, Jack Swigert (left), Jim Lovell (second from left), and Fred Haise (right) received the Presidential Medal of Freedom.

Anchor Standard Discussion Questions

Discuss the following questions with your peer group. Then record your answers in the space provided.

1. What can you infer about how Jim Lovell felt when his crew failed to land on the moon? Support your answer with details from the text "Jim Lovell: Stranded in Space."

2. One theme that runs through "President Roosevelt's Fireside Chat" is that people need to maintain hope to see their problems through. How does Roosevelt support his message that farmers need to have hope? Do you think he is successful in delivering the message? Support your answers with evidence from the text.

Comprehension Check

1. The crew of Apollo 13 never landed on the moon, which had been their original goal. Why do you think they were thought of as heroes after returning to Earth?

2. In what ways would the Apollo 13 crisis have been different if the explosion had happened on the lunar module instead of the command module? How would the challenges that the astronauts faced have been more or less serious?

3. After the accident, Jim Lovell and his crew went more than three days with little food, water, or sleep. During this time, why do you think they stayed hopeful that they would make it home?

Read On Your Own

Read another historical nonfiction text, "A Meeting of Minds," independently. Apply what you learned in this lesson and check your understanding.

Writing Personal Narratives

If you like an activity, like swimming, you'll probably get better at it, right? But what happens if the activity is difficult? Would you give up? Would you try harder? Think about an activity that you especially like. It might be a sport, a craft, or a game. Why do you like it? Do you want to get better at doing it? Have you ever been discouraged or felt like giving up? How did you keep going? How could you share your experience with others? One way would be to write a personal narrative.

ESSENTIAL QUESTION

Why do people enjoy reading personal narratives?

What's a Personal Narrative?

Perhaps you enjoy hiking, but you once got lost in the woods. Or you like to cook, but the scrambled eggs you made on your mom's birthday burned to a crisp. Maybe you love basketball but are afraid you'll never be tall enough to be a good player. Or maybe you like to play chess and are having a hard time starting a chess club. All of these experiences could be written about as personal narratives.

In a **personal narrative**, you describe a personal experience and share what you learned or describe how you changed as a result of an experience. Or, you can simply tell about something funny that happened to you. A personal narrative is organized like a fictional narrative, with a beginning, middle, and end.

Beginning
Introduce the event, the people involved, and the setting. Include details that will make readers want to read more.

Middle
Describe events as they happen, from beginning to end. Build suspense and interest with engaging dialogue and vivid description.

Ending
Complete the narrative by summarizing what you learned from the experience.

Let's look at a personal narrative.

Analyze a Mentor Text

This is an example of an effective personal narrative by a fourth grader. Read it and then complete the activities in the boxes as a class.

Swimming to Win

Do you like to jump into cold water on a winter morning? Is 5:30 a.m. your favorite time to get out of bed? If not, then don't join a swim team. However, if I had not joined a team, I would still be just an average swimmer. Swimming is my favorite sport, but I didn't always feel that way about it.

It all began two years ago, when a new community center with a swimming pool opened in our neighborhood. My older brother joined a swim team and urged me to sign up for lessons. At first, all I could do was tread water. But the lessons were easy, and soon I was doing 50-yard laps, zipping up and down the pool. The swimming instructor asked me to sign up for the city swim team in my age group. I imagined myself heading straight for the Olympics.

On the first day of swim team practice, I thought I'd made a terrible mistake. The other kids could all swim much faster than I could. Getting up early three mornings a week and jumping into a cold pool was no fun. By the end of the first week, I was very discouraged.

BEGINNING The opening paragraphs introduce the author's experience, the characters involved, and the setting. The writer gets the reader's attention by including lively details. Circle the sentence that tells the experience the author will write about.

SEQUENCE OF EVENTS The writer narrates events in time order, or chronological sequence. Underline the phrases that show the passage of time.

My brother told me to keep at it. "Give swimming a chance," he said. "How much of a chance?" I complained. "Getting up at 5:30 is torture. Yesterday, I fell asleep in science class!" My brother just said I should go to bed earlier. Pretty soon, my only friends were the other swimmers on the team. They had to go to bed early, too.

A couple of months went by, and gradually my strokes got faster and smoother. As I improved, I began to look forward to practice. Last March, the coach announced that our team would compete against one of the best teams in the city. She chose the ten best swimmers for the competition. I was one of them! The competition was exciting. Our team didn't win, but I swam my personal best. At the end of the year, I got an award for the most improved swimmer!

Today, I still don't like getting up early. But the possibility of winning gets me out of bed. I've learned that it takes a lot of time and effort to develop a skill. Now I'm trying to persuade my younger sister to join the swim team!

Think About It ▶ What purpose do you think the author had in mind when describing this experience?

Do you think a reader is likely to want to put more effort into learning a difficult activity after reading this narrative? Why or why not?

Vocabulary Study: Synonyms and Antonyms

A **synonym** is a word or phrase that has the same or similar meaning as another word. An **antonym** is a word or phrase whose meaning is the opposite of another word. The chart below lists some synonyms and antonyms, using words from the mentor text. Work with your class or a partner to fill the blank boxes.

Word	Synonym
urge	persuade
terrible	awful
began	
gradually	
mistake	

Word	Antonym
favorite	most hated
average	outstanding
easy	
straight	
exciting	

In the sentences below, replace the word in parentheses with a word or phrase that is a **synonym**.

1. On the first day of swim practice, I felt (bad) _____.

2. The coach was really (strict) _____ and the water was (cold) _____.

3. Every minute of the (difficult) _____ practice session seemed to (crawl by) _____.

In the sentences below, complete each sentence using a word or phrase that is an **antonym** for the underlined word.

4. Practice soon got better. Instead of feeling <u>shy</u>, I felt _____.

5. Some people think swimming laps in a pool is <u>boring</u>, but I think it can be _____.

6. Last year our team had the <u>lowest</u> record of wins in the city. The coach said we can achieve the _____ record this year.

Writing Process

Now that you have read and analyzed a personal narrative, you are going to create your own by following these steps of the writing process.

1. Get Ready: Brainstorm List several activities you might want to write about. Choose your favorite for your narrative.

2. Organize Use a graphic organizer to organize events and details and to plan your narrative.

3. Draft Create the first draft of your personal narrative.

4. Peer Review Work with a partner to evaluate and improve your draft.

5. Revise Use suggestions from your peer review to revise your personal narrative.

6. Edit Check your work carefully for spelling, punctuation, and grammar errors.

7. Publish Create a final version of your personal narrative.

Writing Assignment

In this lesson, you will write your own personal narrative. As you create this narrative, remember the elements of the mentor text that were most effective. Read the following assignment.

Think of a favorite activity. Choose something that you have fun doing, have worked really hard at, or are really proud of. Why is that activity important to you? Did you ever make a mistake or feel discouraged while doing it? Did something really funny ever happen while you were doing the activity? What have you learned from that activity? What would you like to say about that activity to an audience?

Write three to six paragraphs describing the activity and your experience doing it. Get your readers interested by sharing what you know!

1. Get Ready: Brainstorm a Topic

The first step in writing a personal narrative is to choose your topic. Begin by listing several activities that you like. For each one, write why you like the activity, or what you would like to share about it.

Here's how the author of the mentor text brainstormed topics.

cartoons	swim team	cooking
I love cartoons. I'd like to be an animator when I grow up.	Swim practice was really hard at first, but now I love swimming.	Indian food is my favorite. My aunt is teaching me how to cook it.

Try It! Use a Brainstorming Graphic Organizer

Now use the chart below to help brainstorm topics for your own personal narrative. Choose activities that you enjoy most. Describe why you like each activity.

Brainstorm Ideas for Your Topic

You can use a graphic organizer to help brainstorm ideas and details for your personal narrative. Here is how the author of the mentor text used the graphic organizer.

Topic:
joining the swim team and learning to swim

BEGINNING Start by explaining the activity. Get the reader's attention.

Beginning:
jumping into cold water
waking up early
wanting to quit

DETAILS Add details to help your reader see and experience what happened. What information can you add about the setting and people?

People:
my older brother;
swimming coach

Setting:
community swimming pool

MIDDLE Think about which events to include. You can put these events in the best order later. For now, just write down the important things that you remember.

Events:
At first I want to quit.

My brother says to keep at it.

My strokes get better.

The coach chooses me for competition.

ENDING Tell what you learned from the experience.

Ending:
It takes a lot of time and effort to develop a skill.

Try It!

Use a Graphic Organizer for Brainstorming

Now use the events chart below to brainstorm your own personal narrative.

Topic:

Beginning:

People:

Setting:

Events:

Ending:

2. Organize

You are almost ready to begin a draft of your personal narrative. You can use a graphic organizer to help organize the events and details you gathered during brainstorming. You can then refer to the graphic organizer as you work through the different parts of your draft. The writer of the mentor text completed this graphic organizer.

BEGINNING In the opening paragraphs, you

- tell the topic of your personal narrative
- include details that make readers want to read more
- begin developing the setting and characters

MIDDLE In the middle paragraphs, you

- tell events in the order in which they happen
- show what the activity is like and how you feel about it, using dialogue and details that will interest your reader
- continue developing the characters and the conflict

ENDING Your ending should

- summarize what you've learned
- show how you feel about the experience

Beginning I signed up for the city swim team. By the end of the first week of practice, I wanted to quit.	**Details** The lessons were easy. I was zipping up and down the pool. The other kids could swim much faster than I could. Getting up early and jumping into a cold pool was no fun.
Middle: Event My brother told me to keep at it.	Getting up at 5:30 is torture. My brother said that I should go to bed earlier.
Middle: Event Gradually my strokes got faster and smoother.	I practiced for a couple of months and improved. I began to look forward to practice.
Middle: Event My coach chose me as a swimmer for the competition.	The competition was exciting. I swam my personal best. I got an award for most improved swimmer.
Ending It takes a lot of time and effort to develop a skill.	I still don't like getting up early, but I like the possibility of winning.

Try It!

Organize Your Personal Narrative

Now use the graphic organizer below to organize the ideas and details you want to include in your draft.

Beginning	Details
Middle: Event 1	
Middle: Event 2	
Middle: Event 3	
Ending	

3. Draft

Now it is time to begin the first draft of your personal narrative. Remember, your draft does not have to be perfect! This is the time to use your notes, get your experience down in some sort of organized way, and have fun. You will have time to revise your writing later. Start by drafting your narrative on a computer or on a separate sheet of paper. Tell about your favorite activity and why you like it.

Writer's Craft: Using Transitional Words and Phrases

Transitional words and phrases help writing flow smoothly. They also help readers understand how events are connected. Here are some common transitional words and phrases that help to link events in a time sequence.

Transitional words	first, next, then, while, later, during, last, meanwhile, afterwards, consequently, finally
Transitional phrases	on the first day, in the beginning, after a while, the next step, a few days later, five minutes went by, last week, later on, one afternoon (or morning, evening), once in a while, at the same time, as a result, at the end

The author of the mentor text uses transitional words and phrases to begin her second, third, and fifth paragraphs.

TRANSITIONAL PHRASES Read this section of the mentor text. Circle the transitional phrase that introduces the event. Underline the other transitional phrases in the paragraph.

A couple of months went by, and gradually my strokes got faster and smoother. As I improved, I began to look forward to practice. Last March, the coach announced that our team would compete against one of the best teams in the city. She chose the ten best swimmers for the competition. I was one of them! The competition was exciting. Our team didn't win, but I swam my personal best. At the end of the year, I got an award for the most improved swimmer!

Try It! Write Your First Draft

On a computer or a separate sheet of paper, write the draft of your personal narrative. Remember to use transitional words and phrases to show the order of events. Use this drafting checklist to help you as you write.

✓ A good beginning gets your reader's attention. You can begin with a question, a quotation, or an interesting or funny detail.

✓ Be sure to state your favorite activity in the opening paragraphs.

✓ Use a transitional word or phrase to introduce each event.

✓ Organize events in the order in which they happened.

✓ Include lively details and dialogue that show how you feel about your favorite activity.

✓ At the end, summarize what you learned from the experience. Try to write an ending that your readers will remember.

Tips for Writing Your First Draft

- Talk with a classmate about your topic. Explain what you like about your favorite activity. Encourage the classmate to ask you questions. This is a great warm-up to get you started!

- Write down key phrases and ideas before you begin writing.

- In a personal narrative, your feelings are especially important, so think about why you chose your topic. Fill in these details when you revise and edit later.

4. Peer Review

After you finish your draft, work with a partner to review each other's drafts. Here is a draft of the mentor text. Read it with your partner. Together, answer the questions in the boxes. Then we'll see how the writer's classmate evaluated the draft.

BEGINNING In her draft, the writer does not explain her personal feelings about swimming. Is she sorry that she joined the swim team?

MIDDLE Transitional words and phrases make the order of events clearer. What transitional word or phrase could you add to the second paragraph?

What word or phrase could you add to the beginning of the third paragraph?

ENDING The conclusion does not really summarize what the writer learned from the experience. How would you summarize what the writer learned?

An Early Draft:

Swim Team

If you don't like hard work, don't join a swim team. Being on a swim team is tough. You have to get up really early. It can be difficult to stay awake in school. Better think twice before you sign up for a time-consuming sport like swimming!

A new community center opened in our neighborhood. My brother said I should take lessons. At first I thought swimming was easy. I zipped up and down the pool. The instructor said I was good enough to join the city swim team.

I thought I'd made a mistake. The other kids on the team could all swim much faster than I could. We had to get up for practice at 5:30 a.m.! I thought swimming was too hard and I wanted to quit.

One afternoon in school I fell asleep in science class! But my brother told me not to give up. So I kept swimming and slowly got better at it. It took two years. Today, most of my best friends are on the swim team. But I still don't like to get up early.

A Sample Peer Review Form

This peer review form gives an example of how a classmate evaluated the draft of the mentor text shown on page 100.

The beginning states the subject in an interesting way.	You did a good job of *getting the reader's attention by talking to the reader.*
The writer's feelings about the activity are clear.	You could improve your personal narrative by *explaining why you like swimming. The introduction makes it sound as if you don't like to swim.*

The writer writes events in the order in which they happen.	You did a good job of *telling events in the order in which they happen.*
The writer includes interesting details and dialogue.	You could improve your narrative by *adding some dialogue with your brother.*

The writer uses transitional words and phrases to show when events happen and to make the writing flow smoothly.	You did a good job of *beginning the last paragraph with the transitional phrase "One afternoon in school."*
	You could improve your narrative by *dividing the information at the end into two paragraphs. You could begin the last paragraph with the phrase "Two years later" or the word "Today."*

The ending tells what the writer learned from the experience.	You did a good job of *adding a detail that shows how you feel about the experience: "Today, most of my best friends are on the swim team."*
The writer gives a detail that shows how she feels about the experience.	You could improve your narrative by *adding a sentence that tells what you learned.*

Try It!   Peer Review with a Partner

Now you are going to work with a partner to review each other's personal narrative drafts. You will use the peer review form below. If you need help, look back at the mentor text writer's peer review form for suggestions.

The beginning states the subject in an interesting way.	You did a good job of
The writer's feelings about the activity are clear.	You could improve your personal narrative by

The writer writes events in the order in which they happen.	You did a good job of
The writer includes interesting details and dialogue.	You could improve your personal narrative by

The writer uses transitional words and phrases to show when events happen and to make the writing flow smoothly.	You did a good job of
	You could improve your personal narrative by

The ending tells what the writer learned from the experience.	You did a good job of
The writer gives a detail that shows how she feels about the experience.	You could improve your personal narrative by

Try It!

Record Key Peer Review Comments

Now it's time for you and your partner to share your comments with each other. Listen to your partner's feedback, and write down the key comments in the left column. Then write some ideas for improving your draft in the right column.

My review says my beginning	I will
My review says that the order of events	I will
My review says that my use of details and dialogue	I will
My review says that my use of transitional words	I will
My review says that my ending	I will

Use the space below to write anything else you notice about your draft that you think you can improve.

5. Revise

In this step of the writing process, you work on parts of your draft that need improvement. Use the peer review form that your classmate completed to help you. Also use your own ideas about how to improve each part of your personal narrative. This checklist includes some things to think about as you get ready to revise.

Revision Checklist

✔ Does my beginning catch the reader's interest? Do I state my feelings about my favorite activity?

✔ Are events presented in the order in which they happen? Do they show why this activity is important to me?

✔ Do I use details, facts, and dialogue to explain the activity and my feelings about it to the reader?

✔ Is my ending interesting? Have I told what I've learned from this activity?

✔ Do I use transitional words and phrases to show when the events happen?

✔ Do I use effective punctuation to make my ideas as clear as possible?

Writer's Craft: Using Effective Punctuation

Effective punctuation helps to clarify your ideas and feelings. Too many exclamation points can make each sentence seem equally important. A misplaced comma can change the meaning of a sentence. Contractions must contain an apostrophe. Short, choppy sentences are boring. The text below needs effective punctuation. Can you improve it?

EFFECTIVE PUNCTUATION Add any missing punctuation to the paragraph. Combine any short, choppy sentences. Then look back at the mentor text to check your work.

A couple of months went by and gradually my strokes got faster and smoother. As I improved. I began to look forward to practice. Last March the coach announced that our team would compete. Against one of the best teams in the city. She choose the ten best swimmers for the competition I was one of them. The competition was exciting. Our team didnt win. But I swam my personal best. At the end of the year I got an award for the most improved swimmer!

Try It!

Revise Your Personal Narrative

Checking for correct and effective punctuation is an important part of revising. The paragraph below contains seven punctuation errors. Can you find them? Write the corrected paragraph in the box below. Then check your own writing carefully for correct punctuation.

> This year I learned to dive at first I was afraid. Because the diving board was so high. I practiced on the side of the pool for three weeks. Trying to get up my courage. Finally I was ready to dive from the high board. I climbed the ladder. And took a deep breath. Ready, set go.

Writing Assignment

Now it's time to revise the draft of your personal narrative. Continue working on a computer or on a separate sheet of paper. Review the assignment, repeated below, and the revision checklist. Doing so will help you know that you have included everything you need.

Think of a favorite activity. Choose something that you have fun doing, have worked really hard at, or are really proud of. Why is that activity important to you? Did you ever make a mistake or feel discouraged while doing it? Did something really funny ever happen while you were doing the activity? What have you learned from that activity? What would you like to say about that activity to an audience?

Write three to six paragraphs describing the activity and your experience doing it. Get your readers interested by sharing what you know!

6. Edit

After revising your personal narrative, you will edit it. When you edit, you read very carefully to be sure to find any mistakes in your writing. Here's a checklist of some things to look for as you edit.

Editing Checklist

✓ Did you indent each paragraph?

✓ Are all of your sentences complete? Does each have a subject and a verb?

✓ Did you begin each sentence with a capital letter?

✓ Does each sentence end with the correct punctuation?

✓ Have you used commas correctly?

✓ Are all of your words spelled correctly?

If you typed your narrative, print it out so you can mark it up. You can use these editing marks to mark any errors you find.

┌───┐
| ⌐ Indent   ⌃ Add   ~~delete~~ Delete   ∪ Reverse the order |
└───┘

This paragraph from the draft of the mentor text shows how to use editing marks.

⌐Today,
I still don't like getting up early. But the possibility of
⌃
winning gets me out of bed. I've learned that it takes a lot

of time, and effort to develope a skill. Now I'm trying to
          e
pirsuade my ⟨sister younger⟩ (tr) to join the swim team!

Language Focus: Prepositional Phrases

Prepositions are words that link a noun or a pronoun to some other word in a sentence. The words *under*, *into*, *on*, *in*, *for*, *of*, *off*, *over*, *to*, *near*, and *through* are examples of prepositions.

A **prepositional phrase** includes the preposition, its object, and any modifiers of the object. A prepositional phrase always begins with a preposition. The phrase provides information about the subject or the verb of a sentence, telling where something is located or when something happened. A prepositional phrase can contain a noun, an article (*a*, *an*, *the*), an adjective, or a pronoun. Like all phrases, a prepositional phrase is not a complete sentence. It does not contain a subject or verb.

> Examples of prepositional phrases: in the cafeteria; on my birthday; under my desk; around our neighborhood; of the assignment; through the tunnel; inside my backpack; off the table; by next Tuesday

In the sentence below, the prepositions are orange and the prepositional phrases are underlined. The prepositional phrases give information about the verb *went*. The phrases tell where and when.

Lee went to the museum on Thursday afternoon.

On the first day of swim team practice, I thought I'd made a terrible mistake. The other kids could all swim much faster than I could. Getting up early three mornings a week and jumping into a cold pool was no fun. By the end of the first week, I was very discouraged.

PREPOSITIONAL PHRASES Read this paragraph from the mentor text. Underline the five prepositional phrases in the paragraph. Circle the preposition that begins each phrase.

Try It! Language and Editing Practice

Underline the prepositional phrase or phrases in each sentence. Then circle the preposition that begins each phrase.

1. I arrived at the pool on Monday morning.

2. The locker room was empty, and the area around the pool was dark.

3. No one was in the office or near the pool entrance.

4. Suddenly, I remembered that Monday was a holiday for our school district.

5. I rode home on the bus and crawled back into bed.

To check for correct spelling, use a dictionary or your computer's spell-check function. You can also have a friend check for spelling during a peer review. Now use editing marks to correct the spelling and punctuation errors in this paragraph.

I love playing hocky but I don't like the long practises. after playing for two hours I am realy tired. Who likes feeling tired all of the time. Maybe when I improove I will feel better about the hard work?

Try It!

Edit Your Personal Narrative

Now edit your personal narrative. Use this checklist and the editing marks you have learned to correct any errors you find.

☐ Did you indent each paragraph?

☐ Are all of your sentences complete? Does each have a subject and a verb?

☐ Have you used prepositional phrases correctly?

☐ Did you use transitional words to show a clear sequence of events?

☐ Does each sentence begin with a capital letter?

☐ Have you used effective punctuation? Are commas used correctly?

☐ Are all of your words spelled correctly?

Editing Tips

- Read your writing aloud to yourself or a classmate. This will help you discover missing words and awkward phrases. Ask yourself, "Did that sound right?"

- Listen carefully as you read for stops and pauses. Stops and pauses usually indicate places where punctuation might go. Ask yourself, "Am I missing any commas? Should I add an exclamation point?"

- Read over your writing at a slow pace at least two times. When reading for small details, one reading is not enough!

7. Publish

On a computer or a separate sheet of paper, create a neat final draft of your personal narrative. Correct all errors that you identified while editing your draft. Be sure to give your personal narrative an interesting title.

The final step is to publish your personal narrative. Here are some different ways you might choose to share your work.

- Read aloud your personal narrative to your class or to a small group of your classmates.

- Gather your personal narrative and the work of your classmates into a booklet.

- Create a bulletin board display with your personal narratives.

- Illustrate your narrative with drawings or photographs.

Technology Suggestions

- Upload your personal narrative onto your class or school blog.
- Print out your personal narrative using decorative borders or paper.
- Send your personal narrative as an e-mail to a friend.

Reading Drama

What do you see the students doing in this photograph? What do you think is happening in the play they are performing?

ESSENTIAL QUESTION

How is a play a special way of telling a story?

Consider ▶ Is it better to be kind to others or to be powerful?

How can a person who is small win out over someone who is bigger and stronger?

The Hare and the Hedgehog

by Augusta Stevenson

Characters

The Hare

The Hedgehog

The Hedgehog's Wife

Time: one fine morning
Place: the farmer's cabbage field

DRAMA: CHARACTERS

A drama, or play, is a story that is performed on a stage by actors. The actors pretend to be the characters in the play. Characters can be animals, people, heroes, gods, or even just voices. Characters usually appear in a list at the beginning of a play. This list is called the cast of characters. Who are the characters in this play?

SYNONYMS
A synonym is a word that has a meaning that is the same as or similar to another word. *Hare* is a synonym for *rabbit*. What other synonyms for *rabbit* do you know?

DRAMA: SETTING
The place and time where a story happens is called the setting. The place can be real or imaginary, and the time can be in the past, present, or future. How does the author describe the play's setting?

(The Hedgehog and his Wife are walking in the field.)

1   **Hedgehog:** These cabbages are growing well.

Wife: They are very fine indeed.

Hedgehog: We can feed on them all summer.

Wife: Yes, if the hares will let us.

5   **Hedgehog:** Oh, there is enough for all of us—hares, hedgehogs, and farmer.

Wife: Yes, if the hares will think that, too.

Hedgehog: Well, we will let them alone as we have always done.

Wife: But they will not let us alone. Yesterday they called me names while I was eating here.

Hedgehog: What did they say to you?

10 **Wife:** Oh, such things as "Short-legs" and "Duck-legs."

Hedgehog: Here comes one of them now!

Wife: He is one who called me names. I'll hide till he goes by.

(She hides among the cabbages. The Hare enters.)

Hedgehog: Good-morning, sir.

Hare: Why do you speak to me?

15 **Hedgehog:** I always speak to neighbors, sir.

Hare: Speak to your own kind, then. I think myself too good for hedgehogs.

Hedgehog: Now, that is strange.

Hare: There is nothing strange about it. Look at your silly little legs!

Hedgehog: They are quite as good as yours, sir.

20 **Hare:** As good as mine! Hear him! You can only walk with those legs, sir.

Hedgehog: I'll run a race with you this day.

Hare: Hear him! Hear him! Ha, ha!

Hedgehog: You may run in that furrow. I will run in this. We will see who gets to the field fence first.

Hare: Are you crazy?

25 **Hedgehog:** Come, come, let's begin the race!

Hare: Ha, ha! Well, I'll run with you. You ought to know just how silly your little duck-legs are.

Hedgehog: Let us go to this end of the furrow to begin.

Hare: I will run to the brook and back while you are getting there.

Hedgehog: As you please.

(The Hare runs off.)

Wife, wife, did you hear?

30 **Wife:** I heard. Are you crazy?

Hedgehog: Go to the other end of this furrow, wife.

Wife: And why should I do that?

Hedgehog: The hare will run in the other furrow. When he comes to your end, put up your head and say, "I am already here."

Wife: Ha, ha! He will think that I am you.

35 **Hedgehog:** Exactly.

Wife: Ha, ha, ha! I go, Mr. Hedgehog! I go! You may be short on legs, my dear, but you are long on brains.

(She runs to other end of the furrow. Mr. Hedgehog goes to his end.)

(The Hare enters.)

Hare: Well, are you ready?

Hedgehog: I am ready.

Hare: One, two, three, go!

(The Hare runs swiftly. The Hedgehog sits. The Hare reaches the other end of his furrow. The Wife puts up her head.)

40 **Wife:** I am already here.

Hare: What is this?

Wife: I am already here.

Hare: We will try again! Are you ready?

Wife: I am ready.

45 **Hare:** One, two, three, go!
(The Hare runs swiftly. The Wife sits. The Hare reaches the other end of his furrow. Mr. Hedgehog puts up his head.)

Hedgehog: I am already here.

DRAMA: STAGE DIRECTIONS Dramas include stage directions along with dialogue. Stage directions tell actors what to do instead of what to say. The second line on this page is a stage direction: "*(The Hare runs off.)*" How is the last stage direction on this page important to the play?

Hare: I cannot understand this.

Hedgehog: I am already here.

Hare: We will try again! Are you ready?

50 **Hedgehog:** I am ready.

Hare: One, two, three, go!

(The Hare runs swiftly. Mr. Hedgehog sits. The Hare reaches the other end of his furrow. Mrs. Hedgehog puts up her head.)

Wife: I am already here.

Hare: I cannot believe it!

Wife: I am already here.

55 **Hare:** We will try again! Do you hear? We will try again.

Wife: I am ready.

Hare: One, two, three, go!

(The Hare runs swiftly. The Wife sits. The Hare reaches the other end of his furrow. Mr. Hedgehog puts up his head.)

Hedgehog: I am already here.

Hare: This is very, very strange!

60 **Hedgehog:** Shall we run again?

Hare: No, no! The race is yours, Neighbor Hedgehog. And will you please come by and visit some day? I should be glad to see you.

Hedgehog: I shall be glad to come.

(The Hare goes off wondering.)

Wife: *(running to meet Mr. Hedgehog)* You may be short on legs, my dear, but you are very, very long on brains.

> **SUMMARIZE** To summarize is to retell the main points of a text in a short form. A summary of this play might be: *A peaceful hedgehog challenges a stuck-up rabbit to a race. The rabbit is sure he will win. But when he gets to the finish line, the hedgehog seems to be there already. It is really the hedgehog's wife. She has hidden herself there to fool the rabbit. The two hedgehogs keep fooling the rabbit until he gives up.* How would you summarize the play in your own words?

Consider ▶ What accidents can happen to someone who isn't careful?

Do accidents always end badly?

The Tale of Mr. Jeremy Fisher

by Beatrix Potter

COMPARE SETTINGS
The setting of "The Hare and the Hedgehog" is described by the author before the play begins. The author of "The Tale of Mr. Jeremy Fisher" describes the setting as she tells the story. What details about the setting does the author include on this page?

COMPARE DIALOGUE
In the dialogue of "The Hare and the Hedgehog," the characters speak to one another. In "The Tale of Mr. Jeremy Fisher," Jeremy Fisher speaks when no other characters are present. Whom is he speaking to?

SYNONYMS Mr. Jeremy Fisher sees raindrops falling, and then he puts on a *macintosh* and *goloshes* to go fishing. What can you infer about these articles of clothing? What words might be synonyms for *macintosh* and *goloshes*?

1   Once upon a time there was a frog called Mr. Jeremy Fisher; he lived in a little damp house amongst the buttercups at the edge of a pond.

The water was all slippy-sloppy in the larder[1] and in the back passage.

But Mr. Jeremy liked getting his feet wet; nobody ever scolded him, and he never caught a cold!

He was quite pleased when he looked out and saw large drops of rain, splashing in the pond—

5   "I will get some worms and go fishing and catch a dish of minnows for my dinner," said Mr. Jeremy Fisher. "If I catch more than five fish, I will invite my friends Mr. Alderman Ptolemy Tortoise and Sir Isaac Newton. The Alderman, however, eats salad."

Mr. Jeremy put on a macintosh, and a pair of shiny goloshes; he took his rod and basket, and set off with enormous hops to the place where he kept his boat.

The boat was round and green, and very like the other lily-leaves. It was tied to a water-plant in the middle of the pond.

Mr. Jeremy took a reed pole, and pushed the boat out into open water. "I know a good place for minnows," said Mr. Jeremy Fisher.

[1] **larder** a place where food is stored

Mr. Jeremy stuck his pole into the mud and fastened the boat to it.

10   Then he settled himself cross-legged and arranged his fishing tackle. He had the dearest little red float. His rod was a tough stalk of grass, his line was a fine long white horse-hair, and he tied a little wriggling worm at the end.

The rain trickled down his back, and for nearly an hour he stared at the float.

"This is getting tiresome, I think I should like some lunch," said Mr. Jeremy Fisher.

He punted[2] back again amongst the water-plants, and took some lunch out of his basket.

"I will eat a butterfly sandwich, and wait till the shower is over," said Mr. Jeremy Fisher.

15   A great big water-beetle came up underneath the lily leaf and tweaked the toe of one of his goloshes.

Mr. Jeremy crossed his legs up shorter, out of reach, and went on eating his sandwich.

Once or twice something moved about with a rustle and a splash amongst the rushes at the side of the pond.

"I trust that is not a rat," said Mr. Jeremy Fisher; "I think I had better get away from here."

Mr. Jeremy shoved the boat out again a little way, and dropped in the bait. There was a bite almost directly; the float gave a tremendous bobbit[3]!

[2] **punted** moved the boat with a pole

[3] **bobbit** up and down movement

> **SYNONYMS AND ANTONYMS** The story says Mr. Jeremy Fisher "arranged his fishing tackle." What is a synonym for *tackle*? Mr. Jeremy Fisher says fishing "is getting tiresome." What is a synonym for *tiresome*? Would *exciting* be an antonym for *tiresome*?

> **COMPARE CHARACTERS** In "The Hare and the Hedgehog," we can tell that Hedgehog is a patient and gentle character by what he says. In this story, the author gives details about Mr. Jeremy Fisher that help us understand what his character is like. What detail does the author give that tells us that Mr. Jeremy Fisher is getting bored?

COMPARE DRAMA AND PROSE The author uses colorful descriptions to help the reader imagine what is happening in the story. For example, she says, "the stickleback floundered about the boat, pricking and snapping until he was quite out of breath." A play such as "The Hare and the Hedgehog" does not include colorful descriptions. How does a play help us imagine what is happening in the story?

20   "A minnow! a minnow! I have him by the nose!" cried Mr. Jeremy Fisher, jerking up his rod.

But what a horrible surprise! Instead of a smooth fat minnow, Mr. Jeremy landed little Jack Sharp the stickleback, covered with spines!

The stickleback floundered[4] about the boat, pricking and snapping until he was quite out of breath. Then he jumped back into the water.

And a shoal[5] of other little fishes put their heads out, and laughed at Mr. Jeremy Fisher.

And while Mr. Jeremy sat disconsolately[6] on the edge of his boat—sucking his sore fingers and peering down into the water—a much worse thing happened; a really frightful thing it would have been, if Mr. Jeremy had not been wearing a macintosh!

25   A great big enormous trout came up—ker-pflop-p-p-p! with a splash—and it seized Mr. Jeremy with a snap, "Ow! Ow! Ow!"—and then it turned and dived down to the bottom of the pond!

---

[4] **floundered** moved clumsily

[5] **shoal** a large group

[6] **disconsolately** sadly

But the trout was so displeased with the taste of the macintosh, that in less than half a minute it spat him out again; and the only thing it swallowed was Mr. Jeremy's goloshes.

Mr. Jeremy bounced up to the surface of the water, like a cork and the bubbles out of a soda water bottle; and he swam with all his might to the edge of the pond.

He scrambled out on the first bank he came to, and he hopped home across the meadow with his macintosh all in tatters.

"What a mercy that was not a pike!" said Mr. Jeremy Fisher. "I have lost my rod and basket; but it does not much matter, for I am sure I should never have dared to go fishing again!"

30   He put some sticking plaster[7] on his fingers, and his friends both came to dinner. He could not offer them fish, but he had something else in his larder.

Sir Isaac Newton wore his black and gold waistcoat.

And Mr. Alderman Ptolemy Tortoise brought a salad with him in a string bag.

And instead of a nice dish of minnows—they had a roasted grasshopper with lady-bird sauce; which frogs consider a beautiful treat; but *I* think it must have been nasty!

[7] **plaster** adhesive bandages

> **SUMMARIZE**
> A summary of this story might be: *A frog went fishing to catch some minnows for dinner. Instead of catching minnows, he was nearly eaten by a trout. He went home and had grasshopper for dinner instead.* How would you summarize the story in your own words?

The End

Comprehension Check

Think about how setting, character, dialogue, and plot are presented differently in the drama and the story you have read. How does the author of the play present the setting? How does the author of the story present the setting? Fill out the chart below to compare and contrast how the authors present these different story elements.

Story Elements	The Hare and the Hedgehog	The Tale of Mr. Jeremy Fisher
setting	The setting is described before anything happens in the play.	The setting is described at the beginning and throughout the story.
characters		
dialogue		
plot		

Vocabulary

Use the word map below to help you define and use one of the highlighted vocabulary words from the Share and Learn reading or another word your teacher assigns you.

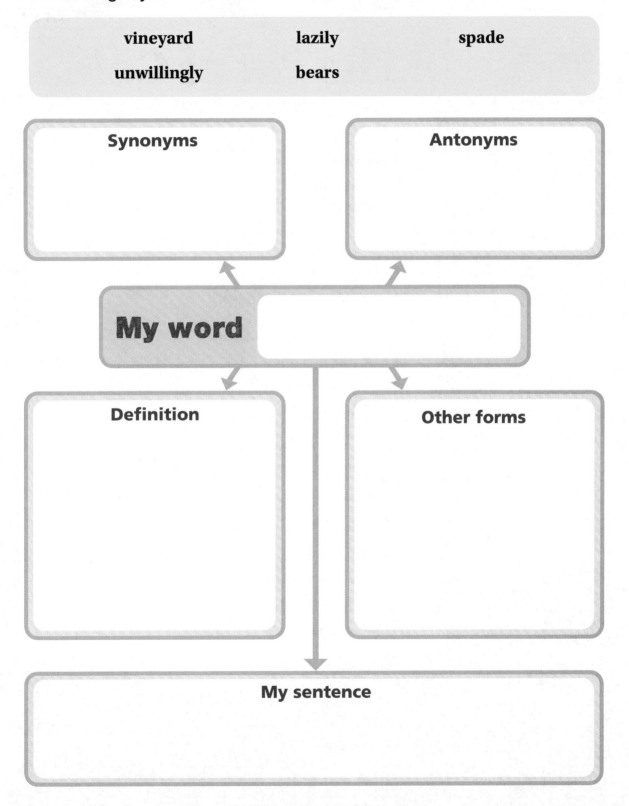

vineyard	lazily	spade
unwillingly	bears	

Synonyms

Antonyms

My word

Definition

Other forms

My sentence

Consider ▶ Can a lazy person learn to work hard?

How would you teach someone the value of hard work?

CONTEXT CLUES
What do the characters say and do that suggest what a *spade* is?

_____

_____

_____

DRAMA What part of the text tells you that the sons do not see the farmer when he enters? Underline this part of the text. On the lines below, write what this part of the play is called.

_____

_____

_____

The Pot of Gold
by Augusta Stevenson

Characters
The Farmer
His Three Sons
Merchant

Scene I

Time: one spring day

Place: the farmer's vineyard

(The Three Sons dig lazily among the vines.)

1 **First Son:** Oh, I am tired of digging! Come, brothers, let us sit and talk!

(He throws down his spade and sits.)

Second Son: Father said we should dig at every vine. But I must say I am tired of it.

(He throws down his spade and sits.)

Third Son: I was tired when we began.

(He throws down his spade and sits. The Farmer enters. His sons do not see him.)

First Son: Now I should like to go to war and ride a great white horse.

5 **Second Son:** I should like to be a prince. I would do nothing all day long but wear my golden crown.

Third Son: I want to find a purse of gold. I would never work again, I tell you!

(The farmer shakes his head sadly.)

Farmer: My sons, these vines have not been dug about. Come, do this work as I have told you.

(The Three Sons take up their spades, but unwillingly.)

Now listen: a pot of gold is hidden in this vineyard. It is buried deep beneath these vines.

Sons: A pot of gold!

Farmer: It is all I have to leave you. I think it best to tell you now, for I cannot live much longer.

10 **First Son:** Why do you hide the gold, my father?

Farmer: That you may dig for it.

Second Son: Why do you hide it in the ground?

Farmer: That you may dig for it.

Third Son: Why don't you tell us where it is?

15 **Farmer:** That you may dig for it.

(He goes.)

Sons: A pot of gold!

First Son: Now I shall go to war and ride a great white horse!

Second Son: Now I shall marry a princess and wear her golden crown!

Third Son: Now I shall find my purse of gold and never work again!

PLOT How does the farmer convince the three sons to dig around all of the vines in all of the parts of the vineyard?

_____

_____

_____

MAKE INFERENCES
Does the story answer the sons' question of whether a pot of gold is really buried under one of the vines? What can you infer about this, and how?

_____

_____

_____

Scene II

Time: one month later

Place: the vineyard

(The ground is completely dug up. The First Son is seen digging. He throws down his spade, showing disappointment.)

20 **First Son:** I cannot find it!

(Enter Second Son with his spade.)

Did you find it?

Second Son: No, and I have dug up every inch of our western vineyard.

(Enter Third Son with his spade.)

First and Second Sons: Did you find it?

Third Son: No, and I have dug up every inch of the eastern vineyard.

First Son: Well, you see what I have done here.

25 **Second Son:** Not a vine that has not been dug about!

Third Son: I cannot understand it!

First Son: The day our father died, he spoke again of the pot of gold.

Second Son: And told us again to dig for it.

Third Son: I cannot understand it.

(They go, shaking their heads sadly.)

Scene III

Time: six months later

Place: the vineyard

(The Merchant enters the vineyard with the Three Sons.)

30 **Merchant:** You say your grapes are ripe?

First Son: They are ripe and ready to sell, sir.

Second Son: Come, now, and look at them.

(They cross to the vines.)

Merchant: Why, I have never seen such grapes as these!

Third Son: We have never had such grapes before, sir.

COMPARE DRAMA AND PROSE How might this story differ if it were written as a short story instead of a drama?

_____

_____

_____

CHARACTER The farmer tells the sons that there is a pot of gold in the vineyard, but they cannot find it. In what way is the farmer telling the truth, even though a pot of gold cannot be found in the ground?

_____

_____

_____

SUMMARIZE

Summarize the events of "The Pot of Gold."

_____

_____

_____

35 **Merchant:** How fine and large they are!

First Son: And sweet, too! Just taste one, sir!

Merchant: *(eating a grape)* Are they all like these?

Second Son: Every vine bears just such grapes.

Merchant: I must have your grapes. I will give a pot of gold for them.

40 **Sons:** A pot of gold!

Merchant: Come, will you sell?

Sons: Aye, sir!

Merchant: Then tomorrow I will bring the pot of gold and take away the grapes.

(He goes.)

Sons: A pot of gold!

45 **First Son:** I wonder if that was father's pot of gold.

Second Son: I almost think it was.

Third Son: I wonder now, I wonder . . .

First Son: No war horse for me! I will stay and dig again for gold!

Second Son: No prince's crown for me! I will stay and dig here, too!

50 **Third Son:** I have found my purse of gold! I will stay and find another!

Anchor Standard Discussion Question

Discuss the following question with your peer group. Then record your answers in the space provided.

1. How might "The Pot of Gold" be structured if it were written as a story rather than as a drama? Outline a prose version of the play, and explain why you structured it the way you did.

Comprehension Check

1. Which character do you think is more clever—the hedgehog in "The Hare and the Hedgehog" or the farmer in "The Pot of Gold"? Explain your answer.

    _____

    _____

    _____

2. The three sons in "The Pot of Gold" decide to stay and dig again for "gold." Do you think they are making a wise decision? Explain your answer.

    _____

    _____

    _____

3. What is the theme of "The Pot of Gold?" How does the author reveal the theme? Explain your answer.

    _____

    _____

    _____

Read On Your Own

Read another drama, "Taking Action," independently. Apply what you learned in this lesson and check your understanding.

Reading Poetry

Look at this photograph of a young person enjoying a water adventure.

How do you think this person is feeling?
How could a poem communicate that feeling?

ESSENTIAL QUESTION

How does poetry help us communicate ideas and feelings about the world?

Consider ▶ How can two poems communicate completely different feelings about the wind?

How does poetry use rhythm and rhyme to create a mood?

POETRY Poetry is writing that uses carefully chosen words to communicate ideas and feelings. The lines of a poem are usually short and organized in verses, also called stanzas. Why do you think the writer decided to describe windy nights in a poem instead of prose?

RHYTHM AND METER Poems have different sound patterns. The rhythm of a poem refers to its beat, or pattern of sounds. This pattern is created by sounds that repeat and by the stress, or emphasis, placed on certain words or syllables. The pattern of strong and weak stresses in a poem is called its meter. Reread the last line of the first stanza of the poem. The line has four strong stresses. Try clapping the line to hear the meter. Which words are stressed?

Windy Nights

by Robert Louis Stevenson

1   Whenever the moon and stars are set,

       Whenever the wind is high,

       All night long in the dark and wet,

       A man goes riding by.

5   Late in the night when the fires are out,

       Why does he gallop and gallop about?

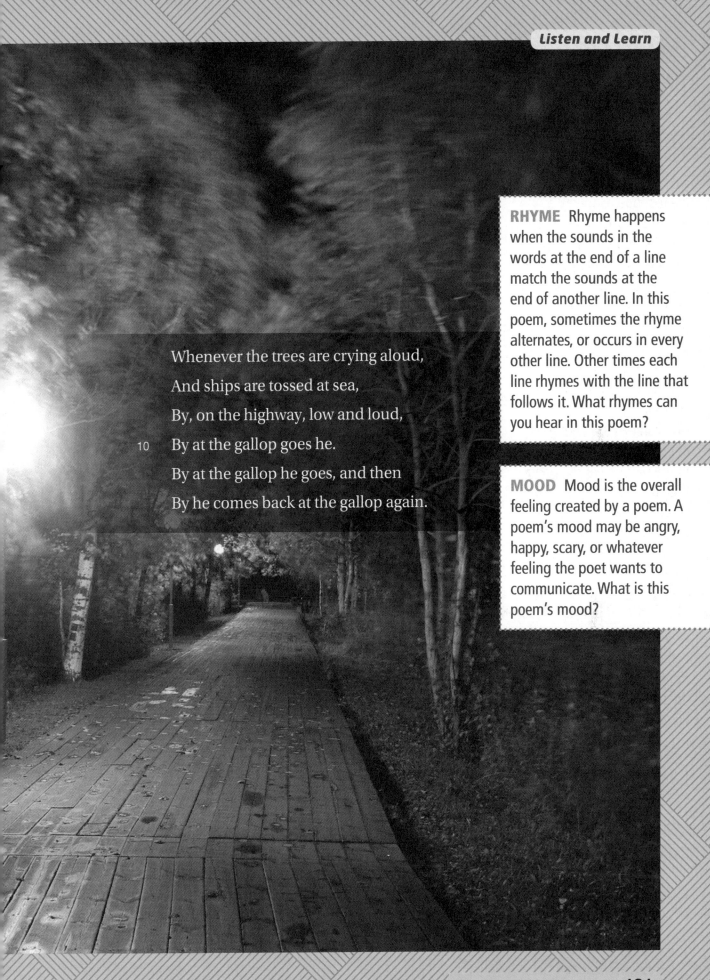

Whenever the trees are crying aloud,
And ships are tossed at sea,
By, on the highway, low and loud,
10   By at the gallop goes he.
By at the gallop he goes, and then
By he comes back at the gallop again.

RHYME Rhyme happens when the sounds in the words at the end of a line match the sounds at the end of another line. In this poem, sometimes the rhyme alternates, or occurs in every other line. Other times each line rhymes with the line that follows it. What rhymes can you hear in this poem?

MOOD Mood is the overall feeling created by a poem. A poem's mood may be angry, happy, scary, or whatever feeling the poet wants to communicate. What is this poem's mood?

Wind

by Amy Lowell

RHYME Rhyming words in most poems follow a repeated pattern. What is the rhyming pattern in this poem? How is the pattern of rhyme in this poem the same as the pattern in the previous poem? How is it different?

CONTEXT CLUES Context clues are words or phrases that can help you figure out what a word means. In the first line of the poem, the poet says that the wind shouts. Look at the context clues. What do you think the poet mean by saying that the wind shouts?

WORD MEANING A rover is someone who wanders from place to place. Why does the poet describe the wind as a rover?

1   He shouts in the sails of the ships at sea,

He steals the down [1] from the honeybee,

He makes the forest trees rustle and sing,

He twirls my kite till it breaks its string.

5   Laughing, dancing, sunny wind,

Whistling, howling, rainy wind,

North, South, East and West,

Each is the wind I like the best.

He calls up the fog and hides the hills,

10   He whirls the wings of the great windmills,

The weathercocks [2] love him and turn to discover

His whereabouts—but he's gone, the rover!

Laughing, dancing, sunny wind,

Whistling, howling, rainy wind,

15   North, South, East and West,

Each is the wind I like the best.

[1] **down** pollen
[2] **weathercocks** a weathervane shaped like a rooster

The pine trees toss him their cones with glee,

The flowers bend low in courtesy,

Each wave flings up a shower of pearls,

20 The flag in front of the school unfurls.

Laughing, dancing, sunny wind,

Whistling, howling, rainy wind,

North, South, East and West,

Each is the wind I like the best.

FIGURATIVE LANGUAGE
Figurative language is language used in a way that is different from a word or phrase's usual meaning. It is used to create a picture in the reader's mind or to make a comparison that helps the reader see ordinary things in a new way. To what does the poet compare the wind in this poem?

PERSONIFICATION
Personification is a kind of figurative language that gives human feelings and actions to something that is not human. The "he" in this poem is the wind. The poet says the wind "shouts" and "steals." What are some of the other human-like things the poet says the wind can do?

MOOD The poet says she likes all kinds of wind. The word *glee* communicates a positive, happy mood. What other words suggest a positive mood in this poem?

How can a poem tell a story?

What different ideas about friendship do the authors of the next two poems convey?

CONTEXT CLUES

Sometimes context clues are not directly around the word you need to figure out. Use context clues to figure out the meaning of *ferocious* in the first line of the poem.

FIGURATIVE LANGUAGE

The hen "says the most insulting things," as if the hen could talk and were a person. How is the clucking of an angry hen similar to a person shouting insults?

The Hen

by Alfred, Lord Tennyson

1   The Hen is a ferocious fowl,
     She pecks you till she makes you howl.

     And all the time she flaps her wings,
     And says the most insulting things.

5   And when you try to take her eggs,
     She bites pieces from your legs.

     The only safe way to get these,
     Is to creep on your hands and knees.

In the meanwhile a friend must hide,

10 And jump out on the other side.

And then you snatch the eggs and run,
While she pursues the other one.

The difficulty is to find
A trusty friend who will not mind.

THEME The theme of a poem is the message it conveys. This poem is about an angry hen, but it is also about friendship. What does the poet want his friend to do for him? Why do you think the poet has difficulty finding a trusty, reliable friend? What is the theme, or message, of the poem?

RHYME Words can rhyme even though they have different spellings. Which words rhyme even though they are not spelled the same way?

The Arrow and the Song

by Henry Wadsworth Longfellow

1   I shot an arrow into the air,
    It fell to earth, I knew not where;
    For, so swiftly it flew, the sight
    Could not follow it in its flight.

5   I breathed a song into the air,
    It fell to earth, I knew not where;
    For who has sight so keen and strong,
    That it can follow the flight of song?

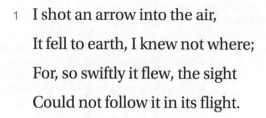

MOOD What is the mood of this poem? How does the poet convey this mood?

Long, long afterward, in an oak
10 I found the arrow, still unbroke;
And the song, from beginning to end,
I found again in the heart of a friend.

RHYTHM Most of the lines in this poem have four strong stresses. Reread the first verse while clapping the rhythm. How can understanding the rhythm of a poem help you read the poem aloud?

METAPHOR A metaphor is a type of figurative language. It compares two unlike things. In the last verse, the poet uses a metaphor. He compares finding a song and finding a friend. How are the two different things similar?

COMPARE THEMES Like the previous poem, this poem talks about friendship. The poet compares friendship to a song, which he finds in the heart of a friend. How does the theme of this poem differ from the theme of the previous poem?

Comprehension Check

Figurative language is language used in a way that is different from a word or phrase's usual meaning. Often, figurative language makes a comparison between two unlike things. Look at the lines below from the poems you have read. What two things are being compared? Go back to the poem and read the lines in context. Then complete the chart below.

Lines from the Poem	Comparison
from "Wind" "He shouts in the sails of ships at sea,"	The author compares the sound of wind to a loud shout.
from "Wind" "The flowers bow in courtesy,"	
from "Wind" "Each wave flings up a shower of pearls"	
from "The Arrow and the Song" "And the song, from beginning to end, I found again in the heart of a friend."	

Vocabulary

Use the word map below to help you define and use one of the highlighted vocabulary words from the Share and Learn reading or another word your teacher assigns you.

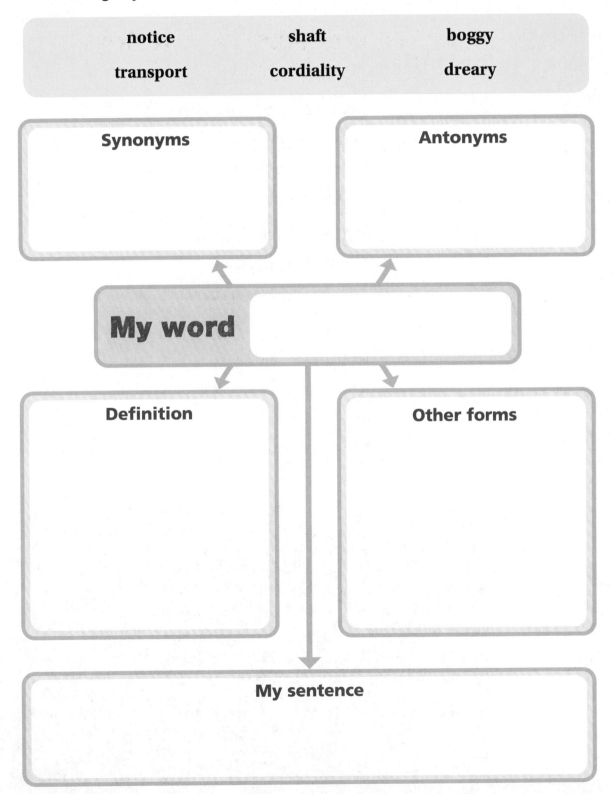

notice   shaft   boggy

transport   cordiality   dreary

Synonyms

Antonyms

My word

Definition

Other forms

My sentence

Consider ▶ What feelings does the poet communicate about her encounter with a snake?

How does the poet compare the snake with other kinds of "Nature's People"?

MAKE INFERENCES
What is the "narrow fellow in the grass"? How do you know?

_____

_____

_____

A Narrow Fellow in the Grass

by Emily Dickinson

1   A narrow Fellow in the Grass

Occasionally rides –

You may have met Him – Did you not –

His notice sudden is –

5   The Grass divides as with a Comb –

A spotted Shaft is seen,

And then it closes at your Feet

And opens further on –

He likes a Boggy Acre

10   A Floor too cool for Corn –

But when a Boy, and Barefoot

I more than once at Noon

SIMILE A simile compares two unlike things using the word *like* or *as*. What simile can you find in the second verse? Circle the simile. What two things are compared? How are they similar?

_____

_____

_____

MOOD What is the poem's mood? Which details indicate the mood?

_____

_____

_____

Have passed, I thought, a Whip lash

Unbraiding in the Sun

15 When stooping to secure it

It wrinkled, and was gone –

Several of Nature's People

I know and they know me –

I feel for them a transport

20 Of Cordiality –

But never met this Fellow

Attended or alone

Without a tighter Breathing

And Zero at the Bone.

WORD MEANING In the context of this poem, the word transport means "a strong feeling or emotion." Cordiality means "friendliness." The poet feels "a transport of cordiality" for most creatures. What does the poet mean?

_____

_____

_____

MAKE INFERENCES What can you infer the poet is feeling in the last two lines of the poem?

_____

_____

_____

I'm Nobody! Who Are You?

by Emily Dickinson

SIMILE The poet uses a simile in the second verse. Circle the simile. What two things are compared? How are they similar?

_____

_____

_____

RHYME Listen to the short rhyming words in the last verse. Circle the rhymes. How do they add humor to the verse?

_____

_____

_____

THEME How does the poet feel about fame or being an important person? How can you tell?

_____

_____

_____

1   I'm Nobody! Who are you?

Are you – Nobody – too?

Then there's a pair of us!

Don't tell! they'd advertise – you know!

5   How dreary – to be – Somebody!

How public – like a Frog –

To tell one's name – the livelong June –

To an admiring Bog!

Anchor Standard Discussion Questions

Discuss the following questions with your peer group. Then record your answers in the space provided.

1. Poets choose their words carefully to convey certain moods. In "A Narrow Fellow in the Grass," Emily Dickinson never uses the word "snake." Why do you think this is? Support your answer with details from the poem.

_____

_____

_____

_____

_____

2. "A Narrow Fellow in the Grass" and "I'm Nobody! Who Are You?" each introduce a surprising new layer of meaning in the last stanza. Analyze how these last stanzas relate to the poems as a whole. Support your answers with details from the poems.

_____

_____

_____

_____

_____

Comprehension Check

1. The poem "A Narrow Fellow in the Grass" describes an experience the poet had with a snake. How would it differ if it had been written as a short story?

_____

_____

_____

2. Describe the rhythm, or the beat and pattern of sounds, in the poem "I'm Nobody! Who Are You?" What does the rhythm contribute to the mood of the poem?

_____

_____

_____

3. Poets use figurative language to help us see ordinary things in a new way. Look back at the poems to find three strong examples of figurative language. Explain why you think the comparisons are effective.

_____

_____

_____

Read On Your Own

Read another poem independently. Apply what you learned in this lesson and check your understanding.

Writing Responses to Literature

If you saw a treasure chest like this, would you be curious to know what's inside? For thousands of years, people have told and written stories about treasures. Sometimes people find treasures and live happily ever after. But sometimes treasures turn out to be not so wonderful after all. How would you react to a story like that?

ESSENTIAL QUESTION

How do you write a good response to a piece of literature?

What's a Response to Literature?

When you read a story, you think about its setting, characters, and plot. Doing so helps you understand the story and its theme.

To understand the setting of a story, you identify when and where the story takes place. You also think about how the setting affects the action of the story and how the characters act.

To understand the main characters in a story, you pay attention to what the characters say and do. You also notice what the author says about the characters. All of these details give information about the characters.

In a **response to literature**, you might be asked to describe and analyze the setting of a story or one of the story's important characters. Writing a response to literature is not writing a summary. Instead, you are expected to write about one or two parts of the piece of literature and explain how they interact. Read the ways to make your response to literature effective.

State the Main Idea	Give Ideas and Details	Write a Conclusion
In your first paragraph, tell your readers the title of the story you are writing about. Then tell your topic, or main idea, that describes an important part of the story.	In the middle paragraphs of your response to literature, give two or three ideas about your topic. Support your ideas with details and examples from the story.	In the last paragraph, restate your main idea and complete your response to literature. You might also add an additional thought about your topic.

Analyze a Mentor Text: Reading

The author of the mentor text wrote about the setting of a story. Here is the story the author read, which is a retelling of the Greek myth "Pandora's Box."

Pandora's Box

Long ago, the people of Greece believed their gods controlled life on Earth. These gods and goddesses lived on Mount Olympus. The ruler of the gods was Zeus. The Greeks told myths about the gods. Here is a retelling of a Greek myth.

His eyes burning coals, Zeus looked down from his palace on Mount Olympus. His anger flamed at the human beings on Earth. Long ago Zeus had determined that humans should never have fire. He feared they would use it to attack the gods. But one soft-hearted god, Prometheus, had disobeyed Zeus and given fire to humans. Zeus had punished Prometheus. Now he schemed to penalize humankind, too.

Zeus dreamed up a mean and clever trick to punish people. He called out to Hephaistos (heh-FESS-toss), the god of fire, who was also a blacksmith and an expert at making things.

"Make a beautiful woman out of clay," Zeus commanded.

Hephaistos agreed. When he had finished the strange task, he brought the clay figure to Zeus.

Zeus blew life into the figure and named her Pandora. He bestowed on Pandora three unpleasant traits: vanity (an excessive love of oneself), foolishness, and an uncontrollable curiosity. Zeus then invited other gods to give Pandora some virtues.

Finally, Zeus gave Pandora a beautiful box made of gold. "This golden box is for you," said Zeus. "You must never open it, though," he warned. "Terrible things will happen should you ever open it."

Then Zeus sent Pandora to live on Earth. At first, everything was rosy for Pandora. She fell in love and married a kind man named Epimetheus. She grew a garden full of radiant flowers. She wove beautiful tapestries to decorate her lovely home. But Pandora could not forget about the box Zeus had given her. In her vanity, she was sure that the box contained some special treasure for her. She first thought that the box must be full of gold or jewels. Then she decided that it must have some secret power that Zeus did not want her to possess. Day and night she pondered the contents of the box.

One night Pandora was eating dinner. She said, "Oh, Epimetheus, I must open the box. This curiosity is like a monster. I cannot help it!"

"Pandora," replied Epimetheus, "You know we must obey Zeus's rule. If we don't, it could mean trouble."

The next morning, Pandora could control herself no longer. She took out the gold box and slowly lifted the lid. A terrible odor filled the room, and a swarm of horrible creatures flew out of the box. Pandora slammed the lid shut. But it was too late. The creatures buzzed like evil insects. They shot out the windows, carrying a flood of trouble.

Zeus's punishment was complete. Pandora had released all the evils that people had never known. Illness, crime, hate, jealousy, greed, sorrow—all the things that break people's hearts—had now become part of life on Earth. Fortunately, Pandora had closed the lid in time to keep the most hideous creature from escaping. This creature would have destroyed hope—the one thing people cannot live without.

Analyze a Mentor Text: Response to Literature

Here is a response to literature written about the story you just read. The author wrote about the setting of "Pandora's Box." Read the response and then complete the activities in the boxes as a class.

The Importance of Setting in "Pandora's Box"

I have just finished reading "Pandora's Box." This retelling of a Greek myth takes place a long time ago. The main action happens in two different places. Understanding what happens in the two settings helped me understand the meaning of the story.

The story begins on Mount Olympus, in Zeus's palace. Mount Olympus is the home of the gods that the Greek people believed in a long time ago. Zeus is the ruler of all the other gods. The gods on Mount Olympus can do pretty much anything they want. Zeus is angry with people and wants to punish them. He thinks up a cruel plan.

The first step of Zeus's plan is to have one of the gods make a pretty woman out of clay. Because Mount Olympus is the home of the gods, fantastic things like this can happen there. Zeus makes her human and names her Pandora. In addition, he gives Pandora some bad traits, including foolishness and uncontrollable curiosity. Finally, he gives her a gold box and tells her that she must never open it. We find out later in the story how these details fit into Zeus's cruel plan.

MAIN IDEA The author gives the story's title and states the topic. Circle the title of the story.

Underline the sentence that gives the main idea of this response to literature.

IDEAS AND DETAILS The author describes the first setting of the story. He then tells what important action happens in this setting. Where does the story begin? What does Zeus do in this setting?

IDEAS AND DETAILS The author provides details about the setting and its relationship to the story. Which details support the idea that Zeus's plan was hatched on Mount Olympus?

IDEAS AND DETAILS
What important ideas about setting does the author give in this paragraph? What details support these ideas?

IDEAS The author tells about the setting but is careful not to give a complete summary of the original passage. A response to literature should be an analysis of the passage, not a summary.

CONCLUSION In the conclusion, the author wraps up his response. What does the author say about the meaning of the work as a whole?

At this point, the setting of the story changes. Pandora is sent to Earth. Earth is different from Mount Olympus because people on Earth cannot do whatever they want. Earth is where Zeus's plan unfolds and all the trouble happens. Pandora keeps wondering what is in the box. One morning, her curiosity gets the best of her. She opens the box. Lots of evil creatures fly out of the box. They are all the troubles that people know today, including sickness, sorrow, and greed. However, the last evil creature doesn't escape from the box. This creature would have destroyed hope and made life impossible for humans.

Knowing that the setting changes from the home of the gods to Earth is important. The two settings show how powerful the gods can be over people. On Mount Olympus, Zeus hatches a cruel plan, while the people on Earth suffer from his cruelty. The story of Pandora's box shows how people were able to hold on to hope even with all the evil around them.

Vocabulary Study: Language Devices

An **idiom** is a phrase that means something different from the literal, or dictionary, meaning of the words in the phrase.

> Ms. Davis is <u>a bigwig</u> at her company. (an important person)
> We spent <u>a chunk of change</u> at the mall. (a large amount of money)

A **simile** compares two things using the word *like* or *as*.

> I <u>slept like a rock</u> last night.

A **metaphor** compares two things without using *like* or *as*.

> When you smile, your <u>teeth are rows of shiny pearls</u>.

Reread "Pandora's Box." Find an example of an idiom, a simile, and a metaphor, and write them in the chart below. Then write a sentence of your own, using an idiom, a simile, or a metaphor.

idiom	
simile	
metaphor	

Proverbs and **adages** are old, familiar sayings that express wisdom. You might hear them in folktales or from people who are trying to teach you a lesson.

> *Actions speak louder than words.*

> *Don't count your chickens before they hatch.*

Writing Process

You have read and analyzed a response to literature. Now you are going to create your own response to literature by following these steps of the writing process.

1. Get Ready: Brainstorm Think about your topic, the main characters in "Pandora's Box." Decide which one would be most interesting to write about.

2. Organize Use a graphic organizer to organize and plan your response to literature.

3. Draft Create the first draft of your response.

4. Peer Review Work with a partner to evaluate and improve your draft.

5. Revise Use suggestions from your peer review to revise your response to literature.

6. Edit Check your work carefully for spelling, punctuation, and grammar errors.

7. Publish Create a final draft of your response.

Writing Assignment

In this lesson, you will write your own response to "Pandora's Box." The author of the mentor text analyzed the setting. You will write about one of the main characters. As you create your response, remember the elements of the mentor text that you found most effective. Read the following assignment.

> The main characters in "Pandora's Box" are Zeus and Pandora. Both characters affect the story in important ways. Choose one of these characters as the topic for a response to literature. Write a few paragraphs about this character. Use details about what the character says, thinks, and does to support your ideas.

1. Get Ready: Brainstorm a Topic

The first step in writing a response to literature is to choose your topic and decide what idea about the topic you want to focus on.

The author of the mentor text responded to a writing prompt about the setting of "Pandora's Box." The author asked himself these questions about the setting.

The Setting of "Pandora's Box"	What's the setting in the beginning? What happens there?	How does understanding the setting help me understand the story?
	Does the setting change? What's the setting later in the story?	

Try It! Use a Brainstorming Graphic Organizer

Now use the chart below to help brainstorm what things you want to focus on for your own response to literature.

Character	Does …	Relates to the story …
	Says …	

Brainstorm Ideas for Your Topic

You can use a graphic organizer to help brainstorm ideas and details for your response to literature. Here is how the author of the mentor text used the graphic organizer.

BEGINNING The author describes the first setting of the story. In the right column, the author tells what happens in the first setting.

IDEAS AND DETAILS
In the left column, the author describes when and how the setting changes.

In the right column, he tells the important things that happen.

Where and When the Action Takes Place	What Happens
The story begins on Mount Olympus. This is the home of the gods. The story takes place a long time ago, when the people of Greece used to believe that gods and goddesses controlled their lives. The gods on Mount Olympus can mostly do whatever they want.	On Mount Olympus, Zeus, the ruler of the gods, comes up with his plan to punish the people on Earth. He is angry because the people now have fire. He orders another god to make a beautiful woman out of clay. He gives her life and some bad traits, such as uncontrollable curiosity. Then he sends her to Earth.
The setting changes when Pandora is taken to Earth. The rest of the story takes place on Earth.	Zeus's plan is completed on Earth. Pandora opens the box and releases all sorts of evil and trouble. She had to be on Earth, because that's where Zeus wanted the evil things to be.

Try It!

Use a Graphic Organizer for Brainstorming

Now use the T-chart below to brainstorm ideas and details to support what you want to say about the character you chose to write about.

Name of Character:	
Things the character does and says	How it relates to the story

2. Organize

You are almost ready to begin a draft of your response to literature. Use the graphic organizer on page 157 to help you organize your ideas and the details you noted during brainstorming. You can then refer to the graphic organizer as you work through your draft. The writer of the mentor text completed this chart.

MAIN IDEA Begin by giving the title of the story and stating the main idea of your response.

Main Idea:
The story "Pandora's Box" takes place long ago. It is a Greek myth. Things happen in two different settings. Understanding what happens in each setting is important to the meaning of the story.

IDEAS AND DETAILS Tell about the first setting and what happens there, and how the setting contributes to the story.

First Setting:
Zeus's palace on Mt. Olympus, the home of the gods. Zeus is the ruler of the gods. Zeus wants to punish people because they got fire from the god Prometheus. The setting on Mt. Olympus helps show how powerful Zeus is. He has a beautiful woman made of clay and then gives her life. He gives her vanity and curiosity. He also gives her a gold box and tells her never to open it.

IDEAS AND DETAILS Tell about the second setting and what happens there, and how this setting contributes to the story.

Second Setting:
Pandora (the woman Zeus created) is sent to Earth. She lives there with her husband in a lovely house. One morning Pandora opens the box, and all the troubles people have, like sickness, sorrow, and greed, are released. Earth is different from Mt. Olympus because people there don't have the same powers that the gods have.

CONCLUSION Summarize how the two settings are important to the story.

Conclusion:
Knowing that the setting changes is important. Zeus plans his cruel scheme on Mt. Olympus, but it takes place on Earth, where the people Zeus wants to punish are. There is nothing the people of Earth can do about what has happened.

Try It!

Organize Your Response to Literature

Now use the graphic organizer below to plan the draft of your response.

Name of Character:

Main Idea:

Details About the Character:

How Details About the Character Support the Story:

Conclusion:

3. Draft

Now it is time to begin the first draft of your response to literature. Remember, your draft does not have to be perfect! This is the time to use your notes, get your story down in some sort of organized way, and have fun. You will have time to revise your writing later. Start by drafting your response to literature on a computer or on a separate sheet of paper. Make your writing lively and interesting.

Writer's Craft: Using Linking Words and Phrases

Linking words and phrases can help your writing flow smoothly, and they help readers understand how ideas are connected. Here are some common linking words and phrases.

Linking Words	Linking Phrases
after, although, because, before, first, finally, however, later, next, then, when	another cause, at this point, in addition, in order to, in spite of, without reason, underneath it all

The author of the mentor text uses linking words and phrases in his third paragraph.

LINKING WORDS Read this section of the mentor text. Circle four linking words. Underline the traits that are connected by the linking phrase "In addition."

The first step of Zeus's plan is to have one of the gods make a pretty woman out of clay. Because Mount Olympus is the home of the gods, fantastic things like this can happen there. Zeus makes her human and names her Pandora. In addition, he gives Pandora some bad traits, including foolishness and uncontrollable curiosity. Finally, he gives her a gold box and tells her that she must never open it. We find out later in the story how these details fit into Zeus's cruel plan.

Try It! Write Your First Draft

On a computer or a separate sheet of paper, continue the draft of your response to literature. Remember to use linking words to connect your ideas. Use this drafting checklist to help you as you write.

✓ A good beginning gets your reader's attention. You can begin with a striking image, a quotation, or an unexpected statement.

✓ Be sure to state the main idea of your response in the first paragraph.

✓ Develop the details about your character that support the main idea.

✓ Use the ideas and details that you noted in Step 2: Organize.

✓ In your conclusion, explain how the details about your character relate to the story's meaning.

✓ Sum up your reasons in your conclusion. Try to write a memorable ending.

Tips for Writing Your First Draft

- Try imagining you are giving a speech instead of writing. Sometimes this can help you find the right words to express your ideas.

- Think about what you would do if you were in your character's shoes. This may help you think about how your character's actions shape the story.

- If you get stuck, do something routine, like taking out the trash. Sometimes your ideas sort themselves out when you're doing something different.

4. Peer Review

After you finish your draft, you can work with a partner to review each other's drafts. Here is a draft of the mentor text. Read it with your partner. Together, answer the questions in the boxes. Then we'll see how the writer's classmate evaluated the draft.

An Early Draft:

MAIN IDEA The author mentions the two settings but does not explain his main idea about the settings. What could he add to make the main idea clearer?

IDEAS AND DETAILS The author does not clearly describe the first setting of the story. How could he help the reader imagine this setting more clearly?

The author says Pandora is sent to Earth, but he leaves out details of that setting. What details from the story could he add here?

CONCLUSION The author doesn't explain how the two settings help in understanding the story. How could he make his conclusion stronger?

The Importance of Setting in "Pandora's Box"

I have just finished reading "Pandora's Box." This retelling of a Greek myth takes place a long time ago. The main action happens in two different places.

Zeus is the ruler of all the other gods. He is angry with the people because they now have the use of fire. A god named Prometheus had given fire to the people. In order to punish the people on Earth, Zeus thinks up a cruel plan.

Zeus's plan is to have one of the gods make a pretty woman out of clay. Because Mount Olympus is the home of the gods, fantastic things like this can happen there. When the clay woman is finished, Zeus gives her human life and names her Pandora. He gives Pandora some bad traits. And he gives her a gold box and tells her that she must never open it. We find out later in the story how these details fit into Zeus's cruel plan.

Pandora is sent to Earth. This is where all the trouble happens. Pandora keeps wondering what is in the box. One morning, her curiosity gets the best of her. She opens the box. Lots of evil creatures fly out of the box.

Zeus plans the punishment of humankind on Mount Olympus. That cruel plan unfolds once Pandora is taken to Earth. These are the two settings of the story.

An Example Peer Review Form

This peer review form gives an example of how a classmate evaluated the draft of the mentor text shown on the previous page.

The beginning identifies the title of the reading selection and the topic.	You did a good job of *identifying the reading selection.*
The writer states the main idea in the first paragraph.	You could improve your response by *stating more clearly that understanding the settings helps you understand the story.*
The writer describes the setting or settings in the story.	You did a good job of *describing Zeus's plan on Mt. Olympus in the first part of the story and describing what happens when Pandora is sent to Earth.*
The writer uses details to show how the settings contribute to the story.	You could improve your response by *providing more details to help the reader imagine the two settings and what they are like.*
The writer uses linking words to show how ideas are connected.	You did a good job of *using linking words like "in order to," "because," and "when."*
Linking words help the writing flow smoothly.	You could improve your response by *adding linking words like "in addition," and "finally" to help connect the ideas about the gifts Zeus gives to Pandora.*
The conclusion summarizes how the settings support the meaning of the story.	You did a good job of *showing that Zeus's plan starts on Mt. Olympus and then unfolds on Earth.*
The writer makes the conclusion interesting for the reader.	You could improve your response by *explaining more clearly how knowing about the settings helps you understand the story better.*

Try It! Peer Review with a Partner

Now you are going to work with a partner to review each other's drafts. You will use the peer review form below. If you need help, look back at the mentor text writer's peer review form for suggestions.

The beginning identifies the character that the response will focus on. **The writer states the main idea in the first paragraph.**	You did a good job of You could improve your response by
The writer explains what the character does and says in the story. **The writer shows how the character's words and actions support the meaning of the story.**	You did a good job of You could improve your response by
The writer uses linking words to show how ideas are connected. **Linking words help the writing flow smoothly.**	You did a good job of You could improve your response by
The conclusion explains how the character's words and actions relate to the story. **The writer makes the conclusion interesting for the reader.**	You did a good job of You could improve your response by

Try It!

Record Key Peer Review Comments

Now it's time for you and your partner to share your comments with each other. Listen to your partner's feedback, and write down the key comments in the left column. Then write some ideas for improving your draft in the right column.

My review says the beginning	I will
My review says the explanation of what the character says and does	I will
My review says the explanation of how the character supports the story	I will
My review says that linking words	I will
My review says that the conclusion	I will

Use the space below to write anything else you notice about your draft that you think you can improve.

5. Revise

In this step of the writing process, you work on parts of your draft that need improvement. Use the peer review form that your classmate completed to help you. Also use your own ideas about how to improve each part of your response. This checklist includes some things to think about as you get ready to revise.

> ### Revision Checklist
>
> ✔ Does my beginning state the topic and the main idea?
>
> ✔ Do I describe the details of what the character says and does?
>
> ✔ Do I use details to show how the character's words and actions contribute to the story?
>
> ✔ Do I use linking words to show how ideas are connected?
>
> ✔ Do I use formal language that is appropriate for this kind of writing?
>
> ✔ Does my conclusion summarize my ideas about the character?

Writer's Craft: Formal and Informal Language

If friends were talking about the story of Pandora, someone might say Zeus is "the chief god who hangs out on Mount Olympus." That is *informal language*—the kind of language most people use in everyday conversation. In school and the workplace, especially when writing, people use *formal language*. Formal language uses words more carefully and accurately; for example, "Zeus is the ruler of all the gods and lives on Mount Olympus." Correct the informal language in this text.

FORMAL LANGUAGE
Replace the underlined informal language with the word that fits: terrible, understanding, plans, unfolds.

Zeus <u>cooks up</u> the punishment of humankind on Mount Olympus. That plan <u>gets going</u> on Earth. <u>Getting my head around</u> the two main settings helped me understand Zeus's plan and its <u>stinky</u> results.

Try It!

Revise Your Response to Literature

Checking to be sure you used formal language is an important part of revising. Practice using formal language with the following paragraph. Replace each underlined example of informal language with formal language.

Zeus is <u>a meanie</u>. He <u>beats up on</u> people because they <u>got their hands on</u> fire. He should have <u>taken it out on</u> Prometheus. Prometheus was the <u>bad guy</u>.

Replace *a meanie* with _____

Replace *beats up on* with _____

Replace *got their hands on* with _____

Replace *taken it out on* with _____

Replace *bad guy* with _____

Writing Assignment

Now it's time to revise the draft of your response to literature. Continue working on a computer or on a separate sheet of paper. Review the assignment, repeated below, and the revision checklist. Doing so will help you know that you have included everything you need.

The main characters in "Pandora's Box" are Zeus and Pandora. Both characters affect the story in important ways. Choose one of these characters as the topic for a response to literature. Write a few paragraphs about this character. Use details about what the character says, thinks, and does to support your ideas.

6. Edit

After revising your response to literature, you will edit it. When you edit, you read very carefully to be sure to find any mistakes in your writing. Here's a checklist of some things to look for as you edit.

Editing Checklist

✓ Did you indent each paragraph?

✓ Are all of your sentences complete? Does each have a subject and a verb?

✓ Did you begin each sentence with a capital letter?

✓ Does each sentence end with the correct punctuation?

✓ Have you used commas correctly?

✓ Are all of your words spelled correctly?

If you typed your response, print it out so you can mark it up. You can use these editing marks to mark any errors you find.

┐ Indent   ^ Add   ⊙ Period   ≡ Capitalize   ∽ Reverse order

This is a paragraph from the draft of the mentor text showing how to use editing marks.

┐Zeus is the ruler of all the gods other he is angry with the people because they now have the use of fire. A god named prometheus had given fire to the people. In order to punish the people on Earth, Zeus thinks up a plan cruel.

Language Focus

Progressive Verb Tenses

Verbs take different forms to indicate different types of actions. The progressive verb tense describes ongoing action. The present progressive indicates an ongoing action in the present. The past progressive indicates a past action that was happening while another one was occurring. The future progressive indicates an ongoing action that will take place in the future.

> I am running in the race.
>
> I was running in the race when I tripped.
>
> I will be running in the race tomorrow.

Helping Verbs

Other verb forms use helping verbs. Helping verbs include *can*, *could*, *may*, *might*, *must*, *should*, *will*, and *would*. Helping verbs describe conditions such as possibility, ability, impossibility, and necessity. *I can go* indicates ability. *She could arrive* indicates possibility. *He cannot go* indicates impossibility. Draw a line to the condition each sentence below expresses.

Thomas could play goalie.	necessity
Marina must go to the play.	ability
Juan can reach the top shelf.	possibility
Elise cannot eat peanuts.	ongoing action
Teresa is writing her paper.	impossibility

One night Pandora was eating dinner. She said, "Oh, Epimetheus, I must open the box. This curiosity is like a monster. I cannot help it!"

"Pandora," replied Epimetheus, "You know we must obey Zeus's rule. If we don't, it could mean trouble."

PROGRESSIVES AND HELPING VERBS
Read these lines from "Pandora's Box." Underline the verb that shows ongoing action. Circle two verbs that show necessity. Draw a box around the verb that shows impossibility. Draw a double line under the verb that shows possibility.

Try It! Language and Editing Practice

Complete each sentence using a word from the box. Be sure each sentence expresses the condition shown in parentheses.

am	cannot	can	could	must

1. Wilma, you _____ clean your room today.   (necessity)

2. I _____ losing my patience.   (ongoing action)

3. I _____ open the door to your room.   (inability)

4. The toys on the floor _____ cause an accident.   (possibility)

5. You _____ store your toys on the shelves.   (ability)

Each of the underlined verbs in this paragraph is incorrect. Use editing marks to correct the verbs by adding an ending or a helping verb.

Wilma <u>was clean</u> her room. She found a golden box. "This box <u>not</u> <u>contain</u> a swarm of evil troubles," Wilma thought. "That <u>happen</u> only in stories like the one about Pandora. I <u>open</u> the box. I <u>not wait</u> to find out what is in it."

Try It!   **Edit Your Response to Literature**

Now edit your response to literature. Use this checklist and the editing marks you have learned to correct any errors you find.

☐ Did you indent each paragraph?

☐ Are all of your sentences complete? Have you corrected fragments and run-ons?

☐ Did you begin each sentence with a capital letter? Did you capitalize proper nouns and adjectives?

☐ Does each sentence end with the correct punctuation mark?

☐ Have you used commas correctly?

☐ Are all of your words spelled correctly?

☐ Have you used the correct forms of verbs?

☐ Have you used frequently confused words correctly?

Editing Tips

• Read your writing aloud. This will help you discover missing words and awkward phrases. Ask yourself, "Did that sound right?"

• Look carefully at each word to make sure it is spelled correctly. Then go back over your writing and read it normally to make sure it makes sense.

• When you think you are finished editing, read your piece one more time. This may help you catch mistakes you overlooked.

7. Publish

On a computer or a separate sheet of paper, create a neat final draft of your response to literature. Correct all the errors that you identified while editing your draft. Be sure to give your response to literature an interesting title.

The final step is to publish your response. Here are some ways you might choose to share your work.

- Create large portraits of Zeus and Pandora. Display these portraits on the bulletin board, surrounded by the responses you and your classmates wrote about each character.

- Ask if you can display your response to literature on the wall of your classroom or somewhere in the school building.

- Illustrate your response with pictures of characters or events.

- Bind your response with staples or spiral binding, or place it in a folder.

Technology Suggestions

- Upload your response onto your class or school blog.
- Find illustrations of the story of Pandora on the Internet, and use them to illustrate your work.

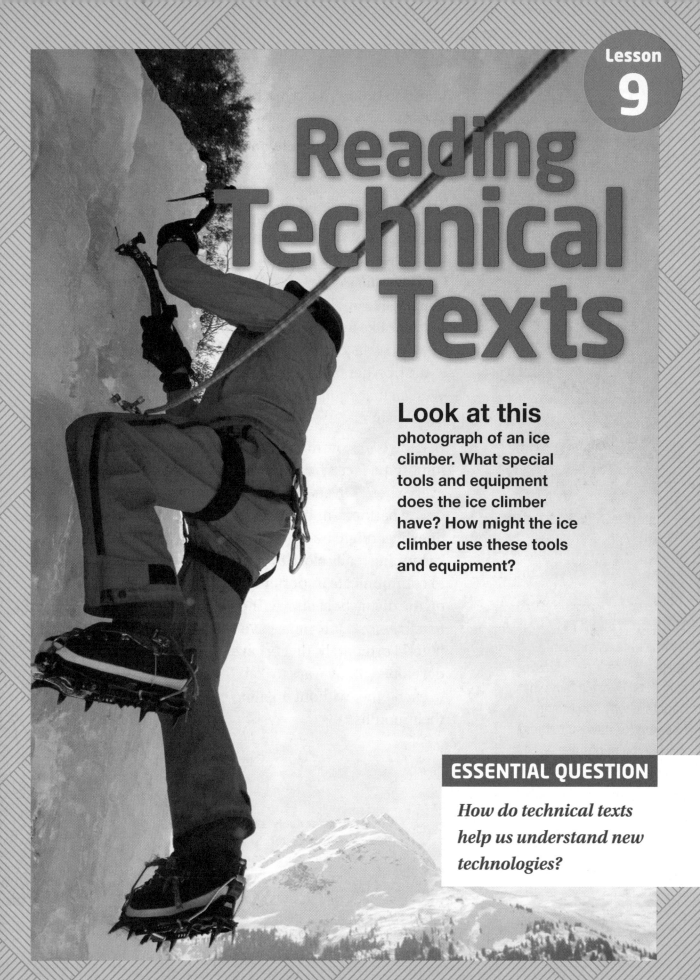

Reading Technical Texts

Look at this

photograph of an ice climber. What special tools and equipment does the ice climber have? How might the ice climber use these tools and equipment?

ESSENTIAL QUESTION

How do technical texts help us understand new technologies?

Consider ▶ What are the different ways divers communicate underwater?

Why is communication between divers so important?

Talking Underwater

1   Have you ever tried to talk underwater? It's not easy. If you try, all you'll get is a mouthful of water. Now imagine what it's like for a deep-sea diver 100 feet below the ocean's surface. A diver wears an air tank on her back and a mask on her face with a breathing tube, or regulator. With all that equipment, even *trying* to speak is out of the question!

However, communicating underwater is very important. It can be a matter of life or death. Danger lurks everywhere. Divers need to share information with their diving partners, or buddies, during a dive. For example, one diver might need to tell another, "Hey! There's a shark swimming really close to you!" In addition, divers need to communicate important information to people on the diving boat above. They might need to tell them, "Don't leave! We're still here!" Fortunately, divers have developed many ways to "talk" to each other without opening their mouths.

TECHNICAL TEXTS
Technical texts explain events, procedures, ideas, or concepts. They explain what happens, why something happens, or how something works. You might use a technical text to learn a new skill, put together a new toy, or learn how other people do things. What procedures, or ways of doing things, are described in this passage?

To work effectively, divers need to work together and communicate as a team.

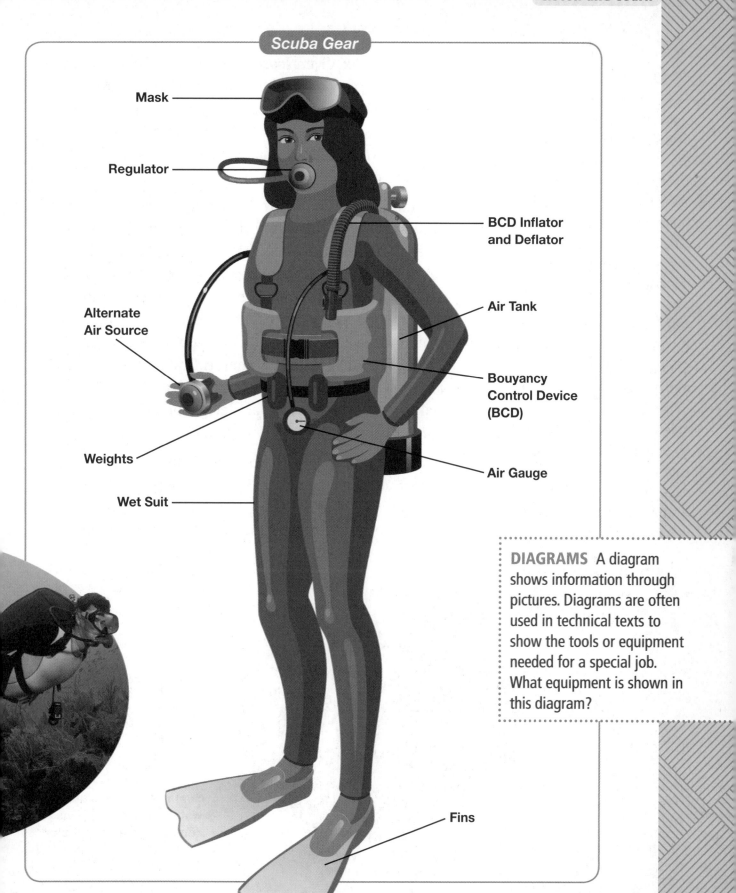

Scuba Gear

Mask

Regulator

BCD Inflator
and Deflator

Alternate
Air Source

Air Tank

Bouyancy
Control Device
(BCD)

Weights

Wet Suit

Air Gauge

Fins

DIAGRAMS A diagram shows information through pictures. Diagrams are often used in technical texts to show the tools or equipment needed for a special job. What equipment is shown in this diagram?

It's All in the Hands

PROBLEM AND SOLUTION Authors sometimes organize text by describing a problem and the solution to the problem. The problem in this passage is the difficulty divers have communicating with each other. What solution does the author tell about on this page?

CHRONOLOGICAL ORDER Chronological order refers to the order in which things happen. Paragraph 4 describes the steps divers go through to communicate various hand signals. To call over your diving buddy, what should you do after you make fists with both of your hands?

All deep-sea divers learn hand signals to communicate with each other underwater. Some divers make up their own signals and share them with their diving team. Other divers use a system of signals similar to American Sign Language (ASL). Divers change some of these signals to suit their needs.

Many diving signals are very basic. To signal "Danger!" to another diver, hold your arm out straight. Then make a fist as if you're about to pound something. To signal "I'm out of air!" bring your right hand to your throat and make a cutting motion. This tells the other divers you need to get to the surface immediately. Other signals are less obvious. To signal "Come closer to your diving buddy," make a fist with both of your hands. Then extend both of your index fingers. Bring the fingers next to each other. Make sure the fingers are parallel and pointing away from you, directly in front of your chest.

5   Signals are useful only if the other divers understand them. Some divers prefer to write messages on slates, or small blackboards, to avoid confusion. They use waterproof grease pencils that won't spill or wash off in the water.

This diver is giving the hand signal for "OK."

Some divers use slates and waterproof grease pens to communicate underwater.

At night, the water can become pretty murky, or dark and not clear. In such cases, divers use powerful flashlights called dive lights to communicate with one another. To signal "OK" with the light, they point the light downward and move it in a circle. Divers must be careful not to point the light in another diver's eyes. The light is so bright that pointing it at a diver's eyes would blind him or her. However, divers can point the light at their hands so that the other divers can see their hand signals.

CHARTS A chart is one way to organize information. A chart has a title that tells what the chart is about. Column headings tell the reader what kind of information is included. Look at the chart. Which hand signal would divers use if they wanted to swim to a shipwreck behind them?

Diver Hand Signals		
Signal	**Description**	**What It Means**
	Fist held out with thumb extended downward	Indicates that a diver is descending to a lower depth. A thumb extended upward means a diver is ascending.
	Forefinger pointed upward; hand rotates in a circle	Indicates that a diver is about to turn around and change direction.
	Upright fist with thumb extended; fist rotates back and forth a few times	Diver asks which direction to go. Other diver responds by pointing in the correct direction.
	Palm down with outstretched fingers; hand rocks back and forth	Tells another diver that something is wrong. May be followed by another signal to indicate what the problem is.

Tender lines serve as a lifeline between divers and their boat.

CAUSE AND EFFECT
Writing that uses cause and effect organizes information by showing why things happen or why things are the way they are. The cause tells what makes something happen, and the effect tells what happened as a result. What would be the effect if dive tenders did not pull on the tender line correctly?

ACADEMIC VOCABULARY
Technical texts often include specialized language that you might not hear every day. People who study the same subjects or who work in similar fields use their own specialized academic vocabulary. For divers, the word *tender* has a special meaning. What is the special meaning? What are some other meanings of *tender*?

Hello Up There

Divers also need to communicate with crewmembers, or dive tenders, on the boats on the surface of the water. Divers can't use hand signals or slates to tell the dive tenders on the boats if they need help. Instead, dive teams rely on ropes called tender lines that connect a dive tender to a diver underwater. Both the dive tender and diver send each other signals by tugging on the line. This isn't always easy! A dive tender has to tug sharply enough for the diver to notice the signal. However, the tenders don't want to yank so hard that they pull the diver away from what he or she is doing.

One group that depends on dive tenders is rescue and recovery teams. These divers search for missing people or for evidence at the scene of an accident. Dive tenders guide the divers as they swim through the dark water. Dive tenders and divers pull on the lines to communicate with each other. To signal "I'm coming back up to the surface," a diver tugs sharply on the tender line four times. Divers also use "buddy lines" to communicate with each other. A buddy line is a safety rope that ties divers together. Using a buddy line prevents divers from becoming separated if the water is dark or dangerous.

High-Tech Talk

Today, many divers can speak to each other underwater using acoustic equipment. However, divers can't talk in the same way people talk on dry land. Divers use ultrasound, or vibration, signals to communicate.

10   This is how the system works. A diver wears a special mask that covers his or her entire face. A tank pumps oxygen into the mask. That way, the diver doesn't need to put a separate breathing tube into his or her mouth. This leaves the diver's mouth free to speak. When a diver speaks, a device attached to the mask changes the diver's voice into an ultrasound signal. These signals then travel through the water. A fellow diver can hear the signal if he or she has a special ultrasound receiver. This receiver turns the signal into human sound. And just like that, people can talk underwater! However, ultrasound equipment can be delicate and unreliable. It can also be very expensive. Many divers cannot afford to use it.

Divers use many different methods to communicate. They use hand, light, and rope signals. They also use special equipment that allows them to "talk" to each other. However, all divers need to know the signals. That way, if a great white shark suddenly swims up behind your diving buddy, you can signal "Danger!" before swimming away!

CONTEXT CLUES
Context clues, or the words surrounding an unknown word, help you understand the meaning of a difficult word. Look at the word *acoustic* in paragraph 9. Based on context clues, especially in paragraph 10, what do you think *acoustic* means?

CAUSE AND EFFECT
When you are reading, look for cause and effect relationships. Ask yourself what happens and why it happens. When divers use acoustic equipment, what causes one diver's speech to be heard by a fellow diver?

Acoustic equipment uses ultrasound signals to send messages to other divers.

Comprehension Check

Look back at "Talking Underwater" to review the problems divers face when trying to "talk" to other divers or to the dive tenders on the boat. Then use the chart below to describe the solutions divers have devised to solve the problem of "talking" or communicating with each other.

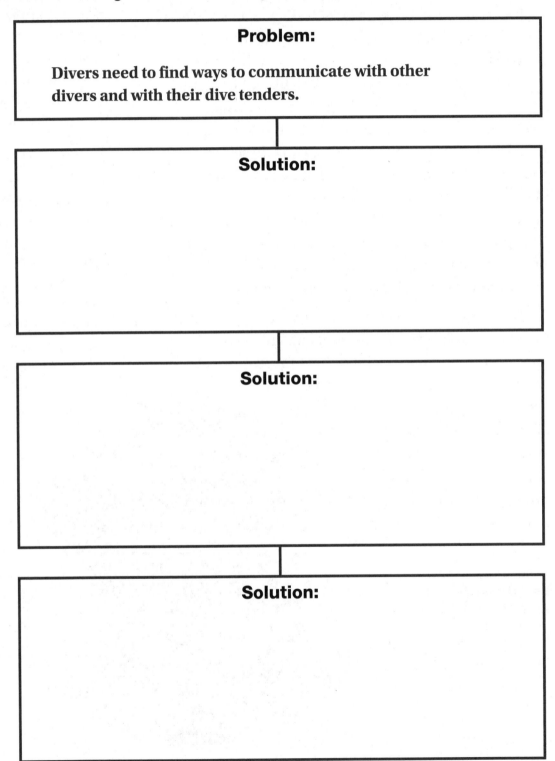

Problem:

Divers need to find ways to communicate with other divers and with their dive tenders.

Solution:

Solution:

Solution:

Vocabulary

Use the word map below to help you define and use one of the highlighted vocabulary words from the Share and Learn reading or another word your teacher assigns you.

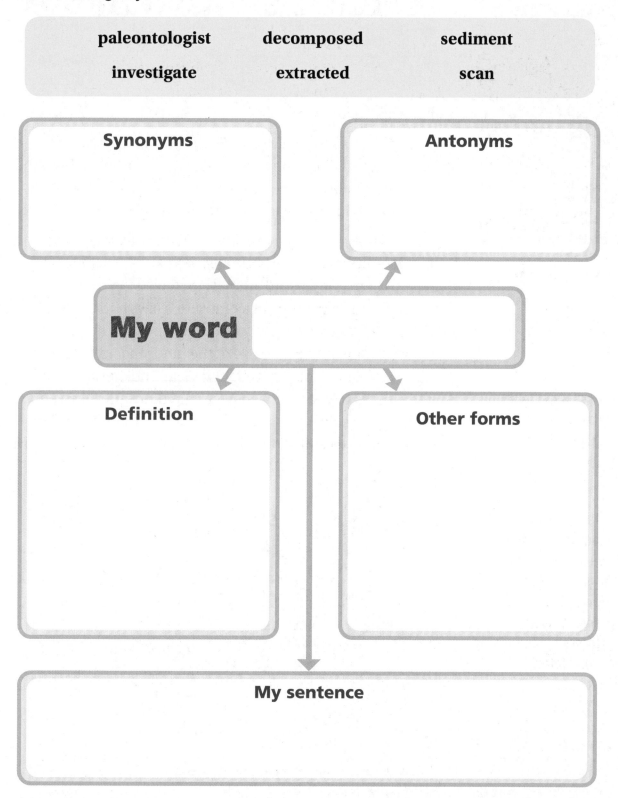

| paleontologist | decomposed | sediment |
| investigate | extracted | scan |

Synonyms

Antonyms

My word

Definition

Other forms

My sentence

Consider ▶ What can scientists learn from fossils?

How have the tools that scientists use changed over time?

Tools of the Fossil Hunter

The Study of Fossils

1 Dinosaurs roamed Earth in prehistoric times. They have been extinct for millions of years. So how do we know so much about them?

One way is through fossils. Fossils tell us what dinosaurs looked like and how they acted. Scientists dig fossils from the ground and study them. Almost everything we know about life from millions of years ago comes from the study of fossils.

Scientists who study fossils are called paleontologists (pay-lee-ohn-TOL-uh-jists). Paleontologists look for clues to help them understand animals that lived long ago. Paleontologists can look at a dinosaur's jaws and teeth to find out whether it was a good hunter. They can also study a footprint to find out the size of the dinosaur, how fast it moved, and how much it weighed. Paleontologists can also study fossils to figure out when certain dinosaurs lived and died. Because dinosaurs have been extinct for millions of years, scientists look to fossils to provide them with a glimpse of the past.

A paleontologist uses a special tool to extract a fossil.

CONTEXT CLUES
What words in paragraph 3 help you understand a paleontologist's job? Circle them.

MAPS Maps show where things are located. Maps have labels and a key to tell you about the information shown on the map. Find where dinosaur fossils are found in the United States. Circle the locations.

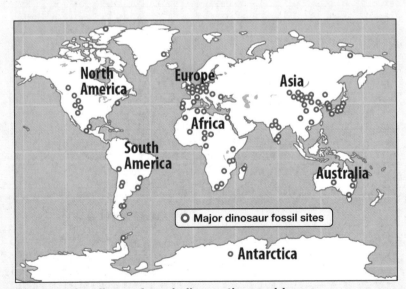

Dinosaur fossils are found all over the world.

So what are fossils? Fossils are the remains of plants and animals that lived long ago. Most fossils are formed from hard things, such as bones, shells, wood, or teeth. Fossils can also be the traces of animals, such as a footprint or the trail the animal left behind as it moved across the ground. Fossils can be as big as a house or as tiny as your fingernail.

5　　However, not all dinosaurs became fossils. In fact, most dinosaurs decomposed or were eaten by other animals after they died. So they left no trace that they ever existed. To become a fossil, the dinosaur's body had to be covered up by several layers of mud, sand, or other sediment. After thousands of years, all the pressure from the different layers turned the sediment into rock. Sometimes water leaked into the stone and ate away at the minerals inside the dinosaur's bones, replacing them with other minerals. Then, over millions of years, the ancient rocks and fossils slowly moved their way up to the surface.

MAIN IDEA
What is the main idea of paragraph 4? What details support the main idea?

_____

_____

_____

CAUSE AND EFFECT
What causes sediment to turn into rock after thousands of years? Circle the words that indicate the cause.

DIAGRAMS
Diagrams are often used in technical texts to illustrate a process. This diagram shows how a dinosaur becomes a fossil. Which step shows how a buried fossil returns to the surface? Circle it.

How a Dinosaur Becomes a Fossil

❶ A dinosaur dies and begins to decompose.

❷ The remains are rapidly buried by sediment from rivers.

❸ Over time, the surrounding material builds up and turns to rock.

❹ The rock above eventually erodes, and the fossil is exposed.

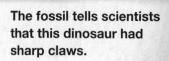

The fossil tells scientists that this dinosaur had sharp claws.

MAKE INFERENCES

Reread paragraphs 7 and 8. From the information in these paragraphs, what can you infer about the size of the La Brea Tar Pits?

_____

_____

_____

CHRONOLOGICAL ORDER Which event happened in the 1900s?

_____

_____

_____

TIME LINE A time line shows when things happened over time. It gives the years and the events that happened at that point in time. When were the tar pits first excavated?

_____

Fossils can be found almost everywhere—on beaches, in fields, and on mountaintops. Scientists have found a large number of dinosaur fossils in the central and western parts of the United States and in Canada. Paleontologists have even uncovered fossils as far away as the Arctic Circle and near the South Pole. Who knows? There might be a fossil under your feet right now!

One place that contains many fossils is the La Brea Tar Pits in California. Here, the animals were not covered with dirt or mud. Instead, they were covered in thick, sticky tar. Scientists believe that tens of thousands of years ago, large animals such as mastodons tried to walk through the gooey tar and got stuck. Predators such as wolves and tigers came to investigate the racket the panicked animals were making. The predators got stuck in the gooey tar, as well.

Over time, the animal bones sank deeper in the tar, where they were preserved. In the 1900s, paleontologists uncovered the bones and discovered that many of the bones were from animals that are now extinct. These bones provided paleontologists with clues about what life on Earth was like tens of thousands of years ago.

Time Line of Animals Found at the La Brea Tar Pits

40,000–11,000 years ago

Prehistoric animals such as mastodons and saber-toothed cats sink into the tar pits.

Simple Tools

Paleontologists follow a special process when they discover a fossil. First, they write down where they found the fossil and what it looks like. They might also use a computer or a library to find out more information about its location. Next, the paleontologist draws a detailed map showing where each piece of the fossil was found.

10   Before paleontologists can study the fossil, they must first remove it from the surrounding rock. They need to be extremely careful because they don't want to damage the fossil while digging it out. Paleontologists use different tools to dig up fossils. You might be surprised to learn that some of their tools are very simple. A few of the tools used to dig up, clean, and repair fossils might even be found in your home or school! After a fossil is extracted and cleaned, it is stored and labeled.

You may not think that digging for rocks is dangerous, but many paleontologists wear safety equipment when they are at work. Since many fossils are found inside caves or on mountainsides, it's important to wear a helmet. Many paleontologists also wear goggles or safety glasses to protect their eyes from pieces of stone as they chip away at the rock.

CHRONOLOGICAL ORDER What is the first step paleontologists follow when they discover a fossil?

_____

_____

_____

ACADEMIC VOCABULARY Why is it more accurate to say a fossil is extracted, rather than using more common terms such as "dug up" or "pulled out"?

_____

_____

_____

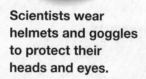

Scientists wear helmets and goggles to protect their heads and eyes.

Scientists use hammers to break up rocks.

Scientists use different types of chisels to remove fossils from rock.

1781	1875	1913–1915	1969	2006
The early settlement that became Los Angeles is founded.	William Denton of Wellesley College describes fossils from the tar pits.	The Los Angeles County Museum excavates the tar pits.	Excavation of the tar pits is resumed to collect all the fossils.	Excavation of newly discovered tar pits begins.

Steps Paleontologists Follow to Extract a Fossil

CHARTS Reread the chart. Circle the words that name a tool paleontologists use to extract and preserve a fossil.

MAKE INFERENCES Why do you think many of the tools paleontologists use are so small?

1. Paleontologists use a chisel and hammer to remove the fossil from the surrounding rock. If a fossil is large enough, a paleontologist might even use a jackhammer.

2. They use small hammers, chisels, and dental picks to remove pieces of rock from the fossil.

3. Then they use wire screens, needles, and brushes to remove excess dirt from the fossil. Some scientists use toothbrushes for this task.

4. Paleontologists may also use vacuums and chemicals to remove extra dirt or rock.

5. They wrap the fossil in paper or put it in a bag when moving it.

6. If the fossil breaks, scientists use a special glue to repair broken pieces. Some scientists believe regular glue, such as the glue you may use in school, works the best.

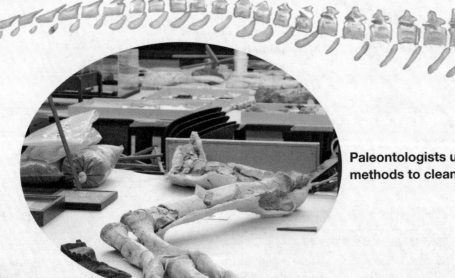

Paleontologists use special methods to clean fossils.

The Need for New Tools

In the past, one problem the scientists faced was that they couldn't see all parts of a fossil without breaking it open. Scientists try not to break open fossils because they need to protect them for future study. It was also hard for scientists to figure out how an animal moved when it was alive. They could not tell by looking at the fossils. The older tools that were used to understand fossils didn't help scientists solve these problems.

Using Computers

We now know much more about dinosaur behavior because of computers. One important tool is a scan. A scan allows scientists to look inside a dinosaur's skull from any angle without harming the fossil. Looking inside skulls gives scientists clues about how some dinosaurs hunted other animals. For example, the scan of an *Allosaurus* (al-uh-SOR-us) skull shows that the dinosaur could not bite down very hard. Because of its weak bite, scientists believe that the *Allosaurus* hunted small animals that could not defend themselves well. The *Allosaurus* made up for its weak bite by moving quickly. Scientists would not have figured this out without the computer scan.

> **PROBLEM AND SOLUTION** This page describes how computers are used to solve a problem that scientists had in the past. Underline the text that describes the problem.

> **DOMAIN SPECIFIC WORDS** Reread paragraph 13. Using context clues, write what you think the word scan means.
>
> _____
>
> _____
>
> _____

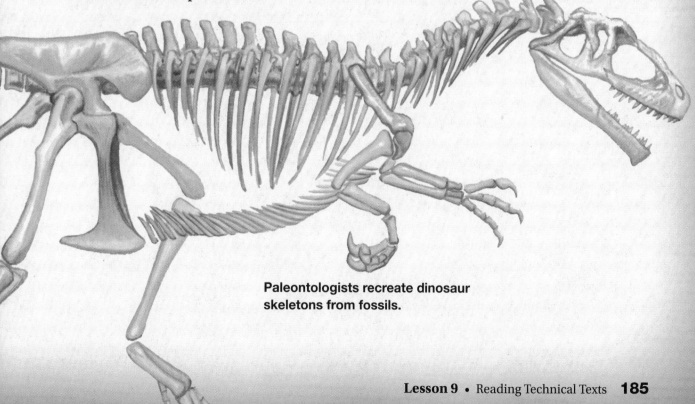

Paleontologists recreate dinosaur skeletons from fossils.

Computer software can also give scientists clues about how dinosaurs may have moved. Scientists enter information about a dinosaur's body, such as its height and weight, into the software. Then the computer shows how the dinosaur probably moved. These programs have changed what scientists believed about how certain animals may have moved. For example, scientists used to think that the _Tyrannosaurus rex_ (tih-ran-uh-SOR-us REKS), or _T. rex_, could run very fast. It's entertaining and scary to believe that a dinosaur could run almost 50 miles per hour. But now most scientists agree that the _T. rex_ moved only between 10 and 25 miles per hour. Because a grown _T. rex_ weighed about 12,000 pounds, its legs were not strong enough to run very fast. Scientists would not have known this information without the use of computers.

15   People have been studying fossils of dinosaurs for hundreds of years. As scientists use better tools, our understanding of the world around us grows. However, even though computers have helped paleontologists better understand dinosaurs, there are still many things that they don't know. In the future, new tools and software will most likely improve our understanding of dinosaurs.

Anchor Standard Discussion Question

Discuss the following question with your peer group. Then record your answers in the space provided.

1. Evaluate the following claims using evidence from "Tools of the Fossil Hunter." In your evaluations, tell whether or not you agree with the claim, citing details from the text in your responses.

   Claim: Mastodons got stuck trying to walk through the La Brea tar pits.

   Evaluation: _____

   _____

   _____

   Claim: Regular school glue works best to repair broken fossils.

   Evaluation: _____

   _____

   _____

   Claim: The *Allosaurus* could move quickly.

   Evaluation: _____

   _____

   _____

   Claim: The *T. rex* could not run very fast.

   Evaluation: _____

   _____

   _____

Comprehension Check

1. What procedures do paleontologists follow when they find a fossil?

_____

_____

_____

2. Which tool do you think is the most important to a paleontologist? Why?

_____

_____

_____

3. Imagine if paleontologists did not have the ability to scan fossils. How would our understanding of dinosaurs be different?

_____

_____

_____

Read On Your Own

Read another technical text, "Don't Make Light of This!" independently. Apply what you learned in this lesson and check your understanding.

Writing Informative/ Explanatory Texts

Take a look around your home. Everywhere you look, there are objects that someone invented. Some objects we use today were invented thousands of years ago. Other objects were invented only recently. All of these objects have an interesting history. How could you share information about the invention of a familiar product with an audience? One good way would be to write an informative/explanatory text.

ESSENTIAL QUESTION

How does an informative/ explanatory text give information?

What's an Informative/Explanatory Text?

Many familiar objects have interesting histories. Do you know how the ballpoint pen was invented? Do you know who invented eyeglasses? Have you ever wondered how the juice box came to be? These are all topics that you can research and write about.

In an **informative/explanatory text**, you present information about and explain a specific subject. The information is presented in a clear, logical way so the reader can learn about your topic. Read the ways to make your informative/explanatory text effective.

Introduction
The introduction tells your reader what you are writing about. The introduction is interesting, it grabs the reader's attention, and it states the topic.

Body
The body contains details that support the topic. The topic is developed with facts, definitions, concrete details, quotations, examples, explanations, and statistics. Illustrations, multimedia, and formatting, such as headings, can be used to enhance your writing.

Conclusion
The conclusion is satisfying and sums up your text in a memorable way.

Let's look at an informative/explanatory text.

Analyze a Mentor Text

This is an example of an effective informative/explanatory text by a fourth grader. Read it and then complete the activities in the boxes as a class.

Take It for a Spin

Today, washing clothes is easy. All you have to do is load your clothes into a washing machine, add soap, and press a button. Return thirty minutes later and *wow!* The clothes are fresh and clean! However, washing clothes was not always that easy. It was only with the invention of the washing machine that the job began to get easier.

The first washing machine was built in the early 1800s. It was made of a large wooden box. The box was filled with water and soap, and someone had to use a giant crank to turn the entire box manually, or by hand. Using the machine was hard work, and it was wasteful. Doing a single load required up to 50 gallons (190 liters) of water. As one inventor later claimed, "There was obviously room for improvement."

By 1875, inventors began manufacturing many different kinds of washing machines. One machine used a plunger to stomp on the clothes. A similar machine dragged laundry back and forth in soapy water. A machine called "the Locomotive" used a drum that went back and forth on small rails. Most of these machines were powered by manipulating wheels, pumps, or handles by hand. It was only in the twentieth century that inventors began installing motors to power the machines.

TOPIC The writer gets the reader's attention in the introduction. The writer also states the topic: the invention of the washing machine. Draw a box around the topic sentence.

SUPPORTING DETAILS The writer uses details in paragraphs 2 and 3 that support the topic. In each paragraph, underline the explanations, details, or facts that tell about machines that were invented for washing clothes.

SUPPORTING DETAILS
In paragraph 4, the writer provides more details that support the topic. Underline the explanations, details, or facts in the paragraph that tell about the history of washing machines.

CONCLUSION A satisfying conclusion briefly sums up the text. What sentences sum up the information in this text? Draw a star next to them.

The modern washing machine was invented in the 1930s by John W. Chamberlain. His washing machine washed clothes, rinsed them, and drained the water afterwards. However, his washing machine was too expensive for most people. It was the same price as a new car! The price of washing machines fell over time.

For a long time, washing clothes was hard work. Over the centuries, inventors designed and made improvements to the washing machine. Luckily for us, today's washing machines do all the "dirty" work.

Think About It ▶ Why do you think the author chose to write about the invention of the washing machine?

What did you learn about washing machines? What other everyday objects are you now curious about?

Vocabulary Study: Greek and Latin Roots

A **root** is the base of a word after all the prefixes and suffixes have been removed. Greek and Latin roots are the base part of many of the words we use today. The chart below identifies some common Greek and Latin roots and their meanings. Work with your class or a partner to fill the blank boxes with words using each root.

Root	Meaning	Word with Root
ven	come	invent, inventor, invention
man	hand	
mot	move	
sist	stand	
sim	like	

In informative/explanatory texts, writers often use domain-specific vocabulary. These are words that are used to name or describe subject-specific items or ideas. The author of the mentor text used words such as *manually* and *plunger* to describe washing methods.

Look back at the mentor text on pages 191–192. Find two words with Greek or Latin roots, and complete the chart below. Use a dictionary to check each word's meaning. Then write your own sentence using the word that shows the word's meaning.

Prefix

Root

Meaning

Prefix

Root

Meaning

Writing Process

Now that you have read and analyzed an informative/explanatory text, you are going to create your own by following these steps of the writing process.

1. Get Ready: Take Notes on Research Research information from a text and take notes. Research visual information about a topic and take notes.

2. Organize Use a graphic organizer to organize supporting details and plan your informative/explanatory text.

3. Draft Create the first draft of your informative/explanatory text.

4. Peer Review Work with a partner to evaluate and improve your draft.

5. Revise Use suggestions from your peer review to revise your informative/explanatory text.

6. Edit Check your work carefully for spelling, punctuation, and grammar errors.

7. Publish Create a final version of your informative/explanatory text.

Writing Assignment

In this lesson, you will write your own informative/explanatory text. As you create your informative piece, remember the elements of the mentor text that were most effective. Read the following assignment.

> One familiar product that people use every day is a safety pin. How was it invented?
>
> You will do some research to gather information to include in your informative text. Write three to five paragraphs telling about the invention of the safety pin.

1. Get Ready: Take Notes on Research

The writer of the mentor text wrote about the invention of the washing machine. Before she could write a draft, she researched her topic. Here is an excerpt from one of the books she found.

> For as long as people have worn clothes, doing laundry has been exhausting work. People had to wash, scrub, and wring clothes by hand. Then in the early 1800s, inventors began creating different machines to wash clothes. One device was a "stomping" machine that used a plunger-like instrument to stomp on the clothes. Another machine used a rake to drag dirty clothes back and forth through soapy water. A third device ran a tub back and forth on rails, causing the clothes inside the tub to bang against the sides. This device was appropriately called "the Locomotive."

The writer took notes on each of the books she found. Here is the note card that she filled out for the excerpt above. What kinds of information does she include?

Main Idea: In the 1800s, inventors began creating machines to wash clothes.
Detail: A machine used a plunger-like instrument to stomp on the clothes.
Detail: A machine used a rake to drag clothes back and forth through soapy water.
Detail: A machine called "the Locomotive" ran a tub back and forth on rails and banged clothes on the inside of the tub.
Source: *The Big Book of Inventions* by Phil Moschowitz

IMPORTANT IDEA On the first line, she wrote an important idea from the excerpt that she was interested in using in her informative piece.

DETAILS She next listed details from the excerpt. How do the details support the main idea?

SOURCE Finally, she wrote where she had found the information. Where did she find this information?

Researching Text

Your topic is the invention of the safety pin. Here is some information that you might use in your informative piece. Read the text. Think about the important ideas in each paragraph. Also think about interesting details that you might use in your informative piece.

IMPORTANT IDEA What do you think is the most important idea in the first paragraph?

DETAILS Which interesting explanations, details, or facts would you use in your informative/ explanatory text?

DETAILS Paragraph 2 describes how Walter Hunt invented the modern safety pin. Which details do you find most interesting in the paragraph?

The first pins were just sharpened bits of wood or other material that were used to hold clothes together. They were not very strong, fell out easily, and could stab the person using them.

The "dressing pin" created by Walter Hunt was the solution to these problems. Hunt owed a draftsman money. Instead of having Hunt repay the debt, the draftsman told Hunt to create something using an old piece of wire. Hunt would give the draftsman all the rights to his invention and be paid $400. Hunt agreed. He then spent the next three hours bending and twisting the wire. The result was a wire with a point on one end, the pin-holder on the other end, and a coil in the middle to provide tension. The modern safety pin was born.

Walter Hunt was an ingenious inventor who also built the first sewing machine. His machine used a needle with an eye, or thread hole, near the point. He was afraid his sewing machine would mean that people would lose their jobs sewing clothes by hand, so he never patented his idea.

(from *Walter Hunt, Inventor Extraordinaire* by D.W. Smith)

Try It!

Record Your Notes

Use these note cards to take notes on the text about safety pins. Remember, write the main idea and interesting details of each paragraph. Finally, give the source of the information.

Main Idea:

Detail:

Detail:

Detail:

Source:

Main Idea:

Detail:

Detail:

Detail:

Source:

Researching Visual Information

When you research a topic, you will discover that information can be given in different ways. You may find photographs or diagrams in online resources. You may find information given in charts and tables. You can use note cards to record notes about these different forms of information, too.

The first example shows photographs. The second example shows a time line. Think about how you could use both to get ideas and details about the invention of the safety pin.

INFORMATION IN PHOTOGRAPHS How could you use the information shown in these photographs to describe how pins have changed over the years?

A Bronze Age bone pin

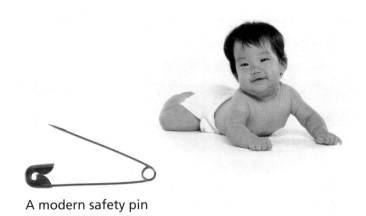

A modern safety pin

INFORMATION IN TEXT FEATURES How could this time line help you write an informative text about the invention of the safety pin? What information would you use?

10,000 BCE	600 BCE	around 1840	1842	1849
Pins made from thorns and bones	Roman *fibula* (U-shaped pin)	Victorian-era pin; easily falls out	Thomas Woodward invents safety pin, but it pops open	Walter Hunt invents modern safety pin

Try It!

Record Your Notes

Use these note cards to take notes on the photographs and time line shown on the previous page.

Important Idea (Photographs):
Detail:
Detail:
Detail:
Source:

Important Idea (Time Line):
Detail:
Detail:
Detail:
Source:

2. Organize

You are almost ready to begin a draft of your informative/explanatory text. You can use a graphic organizer to help organize the ideas and details you gathered during research. You can then refer to the graphic organizer as you work through the different parts of your draft. The writer of the mentor text completed this graphic organizer.

INTRODUCTION In the first paragraph, you tell the topic of your informative/explanatory text.

SUPPORTING PARAGRAPHS In the second, third, and fourth paragraphs, you elaborate on the topic with explanations, details, and facts that support the topic. Later you will include at least three supporting details in your draft.

CONCLUSION Your conclusion should be a satisfying ending that briefly sums up the topic.

Main Idea
The invention of the washing machine made doing chores easier.

Supporting Detail 1
The first washing machines were created in the early 1800s. They consisted of a wooden box that was filled with water and soap.

Supporting Detail 2
By 1875, inventors began manufacturing many different kinds of washing machines.

Supporting Detail 3
The modern washing machine was invented in the 1930s by John W. Chamberlain.

Conclusion
Inventors have made many improvements to the washing machine over the years.

Try It!

Organize Your Informative/Explanatory Text

Now use the graphic organizer below to organize the ideas and details you want to use in the different paragraphs of your draft.

Main Idea

Supporting Detail 1

Supporting Detail 2

Supporting Detail 3

Conclusion

3. Draft

Now it is time to begin the first draft of your informative/explanatory text. Remember, your draft does not have to be perfect! This is the time to use your notes, get your ideas down in some sort of organized way, and have fun. You will have time to revise your writing later. Start by drafting your informative/explanatory text on a computer or on a separate sheet of paper. Tell about the invention of the safety pin.

Writer's Craft: Using Linking Words and Phrases

Linking words and phrases help writing flow smoothly. They also help readers understand how ideas are connected. Here are some common linking words and phrases.

Linking words	*after, also, although, another, and, because, before, but, first, furthermore, finally, however, more, next, then, therefore*
Linking phrases	*for example, even though, as long as, in addition, as a result*

The author of the mentor text uses linking words and phrases in the fourth paragraph.

LINKING WORDS Read this section of the mentor text. Circle the linking word that connects ideas.

The modern washing machine was invented in the 1930s by John W. Chamberlain. His washing machine washed clothes, rinsed them, and drained the water afterwards. However, his washing machine was too expensive for most people. It was the same price as a new car! The price of washing machines fell over time.

Try It!

Write Your First Draft

On a computer or a separate sheet of paper, create the draft of your informative/explanatory text. Remember to use linking words in your writing. Use this drafting checklist to help you as you write.

✔ A good beginning gets your reader's attention. You can begin with a question, a quotation, or an interesting fact about the safety pin.

✔ Be sure to state your main idea in the first paragraph.

✔ Be sure every paragraph includes details that support the main idea.

✔ In each supporting paragraph, include sentences with explanations, details, and facts.

✔ Elaborate your text with visuals, such as photographs, time lines, or graphics.

✔ Write a conclusion that is satisfying and sums up your topic in a memorable way.

Tips for Writing Your First Draft

- Write down key phrases and ideas before you begin writing. Sometimes this is a great warm-up to get you started.

- Focus on ideas, not details. Since you will revise and edit later, you can fix the details then. In drafting, it's the ideas that count.

- Sometimes people write better after physical activity. If you get stuck, take a walk around the block.

4. Peer Review

After you finish your draft, you can work with a partner to review each other's drafts. Here is a draft of the mentor text. Read it with your partner. Together, answer the questions in the boxes. Then we'll see how the writer's classmate evaluated the draft.

An Early Draft:

Take It for a Spin

Today, washing clothes is easy. All you need to do is put your clothes into a washing machine. Then you add soap and press a button. Come back thirty minutes later and zap! The clothes are washed and smell great! Another invention was the toothbrush. The first toothbrush was used in China.

The first washing machines were created in the early 1800s. They were made of a box that a person filled with water and soap. Then the person used a crank to turn it. It was hard work. In addition, doing a single load required "up to 50 gallons (190 liters) of water."

By 1875, inventors began manufacturing many different kinds of washing machines. One machine used a plunger to stomp on the clothes. Another machine dragged clothes in soapy water. A machine called "the Locomotive" used a drum that went back and forth on small rails. Most of these machines were powered by wheels, pumps, or handles. It was only in the twentieth century that inventors began putting in motors to power the machines.

The modern washing machine was invented in the 1930s. It was invented by a man named John W. Chamberlain. His washing machine washed clothes, rinsed them, and drained the water afterwards.

For a long time, washing clothes was hard work. Today, some washing machines have an opening at the top to put in your clothes. Other washing machines have a lid in the front.

INTRODUCTION In her draft, the writer does not have a clear main idea. Is the text about the invention of the washing machine or the toothbrush?

SUPPORTING PARAGRAPHS The fourth paragraph talks about the modern washing machine. What kinds of details might the writer include about the modern washing machine?

CONCLUSION The conclusion does not really sum up the text. How would you sum up the text?

An Example Peer Review Form

This peer review form gives an example of how a classmate evaluated the draft of the mentor text shown on page 204.

The introduction states the topic in an interesting way.	You did a good job of *getting the reader's attention.*
The main idea of the text is clear.	You could improve your informative/explanatory text by *writing a clearer main idea. Your main idea was confusing.*

The writer supports the main idea with at least three strong supporting details.	You did a good job of *giving three supporting details.*
The writer includes explanations, details, and facts.	You could improve your informative/explanatory text by *adding more explanations, details, or facts to the fourth paragraph.*

The writer uses linking words correctly to make the writing flow smoothly.	You did a good job of *using the linking phrase "in addition" in the second paragraph.*
	You could improve your informative/explanatory text by *using more linking words, such as "still" or "yet," in the third paragraph.*

The writer includes a satisfying and memorable conclusion.	You did a good job of *including a concluding statement.*
The conclusion sums up the text.	You could improve your informative/explanatory text by *adding one or two sentences to your conclusion that briefly summarize your text.*

Try It!   Peer Review with a Partner

Now you are going to work with a partner to review each other's drafts. You will use the peer review form below. If you need help, look back at the mentor text writer's peer review form for suggestions.

The introduction states the topic in an interesting way. **The main idea of the text is clear.**	You did a good job of --- You could improve your draft by
The writer supports the main idea with at least three strong supporting details. **The writer includes explanations, details, and facts.**	You did a good job of --- You could improve your draft by
The writer uses linking words correctly to make the writing flow smoothly.	You did a good job of --- You could improve your draft by
The writer includes a satisfying and memorable conclusion. **The conclusion sums up the text.**	You did a good job of --- You could improve your draft by

Try It!

Record Key Peer Review Comments

Now it's time for you and your partner to share your comments with each other. Listen to your partner's feedback, and write down the key comments in the left column. Then write some ideas for improving your draft in the right column.

My review says my introduction	I will
My review says that my supporting details	I will
My review says that my use of linking words	I will
My review says that my conclusion	I will

Write anything else you notice about your draft that you think you can improve.

5. Revise

In this step of the writing process, you will work on parts of your draft that need improvement. Use the peer review form that your classmate completed to help you. Also use your own ideas about how to improve each part of your informative/explanatory text. This checklist includes things to think about as you revise.

Revision Checklist

✔ Does my beginning catch the reader's interest? Do I state my main idea clearly?

✔ Do I use explanations, details, and facts to support the main idea?

✔ Is my conclusion interesting? Have I summed up the text well?

✔ Do I use linking words properly to make the writing flow smoothly?

✔ Do I use precise language to make my ideas as clear as they can be?

Writer's Craft: Using Precise and Domain-Specific Language

Using precise and domain-specific words makes your informative/explanatory text clearer and more descriptive. For example, instead of using the word *big*, you might use the word *gigantic*. You might use a word that is specific to your topic. Look at the mentor text for examples of precise and domain-specific language.

PRECISE AND DOMAIN-SPECIFIC LANGUAGE Underline precise and domain-specific language in this paragraph. Look at the word *dragged* in the third sentence. Would *moved* have been more or less precise in this sentence? Why?

By 1875, inventors began manufacturing many different kinds of washing machines. One machine used a plunger to stomp on the clothes. A similar machine dragged laundry back and forth in soapy water. A machine called "the Locomotive" used a drum that went back and forth on small rails. Most of these machines were powered by manipulating wheels, pumps, or handles by hand. It was only in the twentieth century that inventors began installing motors to power the machines.

Try It!

Revise Your Informative/Explanatory Text

Replacing simple words with more descriptive or precise words is an important part of revising. Practice using precise language with the following paragraph. Replace each underlined word with a more precise, interesting word. Write your answers on the lines below the paragraph.

> Washing clothes by hand is <u>hard</u>. First, fill a tub with water. Then, <u>put</u> in some soap and swish the clothes around. Next, wring the clothes out before you rinse. Make sure you hold the clothes tightly. <u>Get</u> all the water out, and then rinse with clean water. Washing clothes will make them smell <u>nice</u>!

Replace *hard* with _____

Replace *put* with _____

Replace *Get* with _____

Replace *nice* with _____

Writing Assignment

Now it's time to revise the draft of your informative piece. Continue working on a computer or on a separate sheet of paper. Review the assignment, repeated below, and the revision checklist. Doing so will help you know that you have included everything you need.

> One familiar product that people use every day is a safety pin. How was it invented?
>
> You will do some research to gather information to include in your informative text. Write three to five paragraphs telling about the invention of the safety pin.

6. Edit

After revising your informative/explanatory text, you will edit it. When you edit, you read very carefully to be sure to find any mistakes in your writing. Here's a checklist of some things to look for as you edit.

Editing Checklist

✓ Did you indent each paragraph?

✓ Are all of your sentences complete? Does each have a subject and a verb?

✓ Did you begin each sentence with a capital letter?

✓ Does each sentence end with the correct punctuation?

✓ Have you used commas correctly?

✓ Are all of your words spelled correctly?

If you typed your draft, print it out so you can correct it. You can use these editing marks to mark any errors you find.

| ⌐ Indent | _ Underline or Italicize | ⌃ Add |
| delete Delete | ∩ Reverse the order of letters or words | |

This is a paragraph from the draft of the mentor text showing how to use editing marks.

⌐The modern washing machine invented was in the

1930s by John W. Chamberlain. His washing machine

washed clothes, rinsed them, and drained the water afterwards afterwerds.

However, his washing machine was too too expensive

for most people. It was the same price prise as a new car!

washing
Fortunately, though, the price of machines fell over time.

Language Focus

Adjectives

An **adjective** is a word that describes a noun or pronoun. When using more than one adjective to describe a noun, place the adjectives in the following order:

1. Opinion (an <u>interesting</u> movie)
2. Size (a <u>giant</u> tree)
3. Age (a <u>new</u> house)
4. Shape (a <u>round</u> hole)
5. Color (a <u>yellow</u> banana)
6. Origin (<u>Mexican</u> food)
7. Material (a <u>metal</u> box)

In the following sentence, the adjectives are listed in the correct pattern to describe the noun *shoes* and the noun *box*.

She bought a pair of <u>small</u> <u>red</u> <u>Italian</u> shoes (size, color, origin) and put them in an <u>interesting</u> <u>old</u> <u>square</u> <u>cardboard</u> box (opinion, age, shape, material).

Commas

In a compound sentence, two simple sentences are connected by a **comma** and a coordinating conjunction. Some **coordinating conjunctions** are *and*, *but*, and *or*.

Quotation Marks

If you are using dialogue or a direct quotation spoken by a person or from a source such as a book, newspaper, or magazine, use a comma and quotation marks to enclose the quotation.

> The first washing machine was built in the early 1800s. It was made of a large wooden box. The box was filled with water and soap, and someone had to use a giant crank to turn the box manually, or by hand.

COMMA Read this section of the mentor text. Underline the compound sentence. Circle the comma and the coordinating conjunction.

Try It!   Language and Editing Practice

Rewrite the following sentences by putting the adjectives in the correct order.

1. My brother and I watched a foreign great old film.

    _____

2. Thad ate a red round giant apple.

    _____

Combine the following sentences using a coordinating conjunction and comma.

3. Playing a game sounds like fun. I would like to see a movie.

    _____

4. We can hire a plumber. We can fix the leak ourselves.

    _____

Rewrite the following sentences using a comma and quotation marks.

5. The first sentence in the article read It was a great moment.

    _____

6. The book begins with the sentence It was the best of times, it was the worst of times.

    _____

Now use editing marks to correct the errors in this paragraph.

Early washing machines could wash or rinse. They could not do both.

They also had large square motors that often broke. One reporter said

Whoever builds a reliable washing machine will make a fortune!

Try It!

Edit Your Informative/Explanatory Text

Now edit your informative/explanatory text. Use this checklist and the editing marks you have learned to correct any errors you find.

☐ Do the subjects and verbs in your sentences agree?

☐ Are there any missing or repeated words in your sentences?

☐ Did you begin each sentence with a capital letter?

☐ Does each sentence end with the correct punctuation mark?

☐ Have you used commas correctly in compound sentences?

☐ Have you used commas and quotation marks correctly in direct quotations?

☐ If you used more than one adjective to describe a noun, are the adjectives in the correct order?

Editing Tips

- Read your writing aloud. This will help you discover missing words and awkward phrases. Ask yourself, "Did that sound right?"

- Listen carefully as you read. Do you need to take a breath when you're reading some of the sentences? That usually indicates sentences that are run-ons. They need to be divided up.

- Read over your writing at a slow pace at least two times. When reading for small details, one reading is not enough!

7. Publish

On a computer or a separate sheet of paper, create a neat final draft of your informative/explanatory text. Correct all errors that you identified while editing your draft. Be sure to give your informative/explanatory text an interesting title.

The final step is to publish your informative/explanatory text. Here are some different ways you might choose to share your work.

- Read aloud your informative/explanatory text to your class or to a small group of your classmates.

- Create an old-fashioned newspaper that features the invention of the safety pin as the headline story.

- Create a class book that includes your text and those of your classmates.

- Create a poster using your informative/explanatory text and drawings or photographs from magazines or newspapers.

- Create a brochure that includes the invention you wrote about and drawings of it or photographs from magazines or newspapers.

Technology Suggestions

- Publish your informative/explanatory text in a multimedia presentation using digital images and photographs.
- Create a simple Web page about the invention.

Reading Scientific Nonfiction

Look at the storm in this photograph. What would you do if you knew a storm like this was coming your way?

ESSENTIAL QUESTION

How does scientific nonfiction help us understand the world around us?

Consider ▶ Why are tornadoes considered to be among nature's worst storms?

How does a tornado form?

Nature's Worst Storms

SCIENTIFIC NONFICTION
Scientific nonfiction provides factual information about different topics. It explains scientific events, procedures, ideas, or concepts and provides factual details to support the explanations. What event is explained in this passage?

SEQUENCE OF EVENTS
Scientific nonfiction often explains a sequence of events, or the order in which things happen. Paragraph 3 describes how tornadoes form. What happens after storm winds change direction and speed? How does this cause a tornado to form?

SCIENCE VOCABULARY
Scientific nonfiction often uses words that have specific scientific meanings. In paragraph 3, the author uses the word *vortex*. What does *vortex* mean?

1   Imagine that you're inside your home one stormy day. You sit and play a game as the howl of the wind grows louder and louder. You look out the window and see gray clouds darkening the sky. Raindrops and large chunks of hail strike the ground. Then, in an instant, the wind stops, and the air suddenly becomes very, very still.

Don't be fooled. The storm isn't over. You will certainly know that when you hear a thunderous roar. It sounds like a train is right outside your window. Don't look out now. It's time to run for cover. That's because a tall, funnel-shaped cloud has begun to stretch down to the ground. It twirls like a top and travels from side to side. It's a tornado, and it's one of the worst storms on Earth.

The Wind-Up

So how does such a deadly tornado form? First, as a storm develops, the wind changes direction and speed. Warm, moist air begins to swirl in the lower part of the atmosphere. Then, rising air begins to tilt this swirling wind. Finally, the wind is no longer spread out horizontally across the ground but is spinning vertically from the ground up, looking like the drain of your bathtub when you let the water out. This whirling center, or vortex, of powerful wind is where tornadoes take shape.

In the photo above, whirling winds have formed a vertical column.

In this photo, the column of whirling wind has become a tornado.

How a Tornado Forms

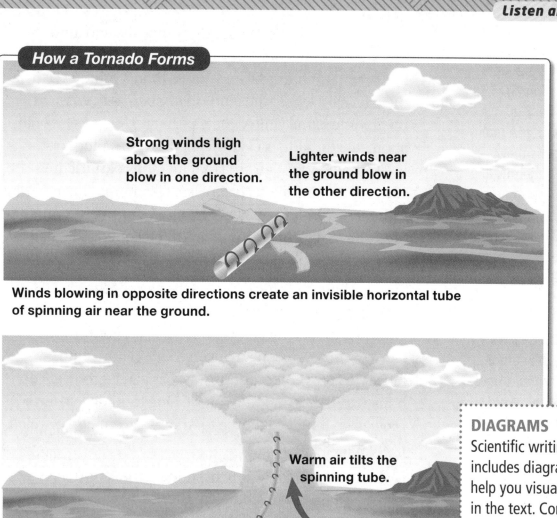

Strong winds high above the ground blow in one direction.

Lighter winds near the ground blow in the other direction.

Winds blowing in opposite directions create an invisible horizontal tube of spinning air near the ground.

Warm air tilts the spinning tube.

Updraft

As the storm takes shape, warm air rises, lifting the spinning tube to a vertical position within the thundercloud.

Anvil

Thundercloud

Tornado

A tornado forms within the spinning column of air. The tornado extends down from the anvil at the top of the cloud. The bottom of the tornado skips along the ground and can cause great destruction.

DIAGRAMS
Scientific writing often includes diagrams to help you visualize ideas in the text. Compare the information in paragraph 3 with the diagram that shows how tornadoes form. How does the diagram help you understand what the text means when it says "rising air begins to tilt this swirling wind"?

SUPPORTING DETAILS
Supporting details are facts or other information an author gives to back up a more important idea. A main idea on this page is that tornadoes are dangerous and powerful. One supporting detail is that the winds can reach up to 300 miles per hour. What other supporting details does the author give?

SCIENCE VOCABULARY
In paragraph 5, the author uses the word *cyclonic*. How can you tell that this word describes a circular motion?

SCIENCE VOCABULARY
What clues help you understand the meaning of the word *velocity* in paragraph 5? What does *velocity* mean?

This can all happen incredibly quickly, and almost anywhere in the world. Tornadoes can form in as little as five or ten minutes and end in less than a minute. Usually, they develop where the land is flat, such as the area in the middle of the United States. That region gets hit with about 800 tornadoes every year. Many tornadoes occur in "Tornado Alley," an area that includes parts of the states of South Dakota, Nebraska, Oklahoma, Texas, and Colorado. Tornado Alley experiences the greatest number of strong and violent tornadoes in the country.

5   Tornadoes are extremely dangerous and powerful. The swirling, cyclonic winds can reach speeds of 200 or 300 miles per hour. Also, tornadoes can travel along the ground at a velocity of up to 50 miles per hour. They act like a vacuum, sucking up everything in their path—fences, cars, even homes! Tornadoes can lift roofs off of houses and tear buildings apart. One tornado carried a motel sign from Oklahoma to Arkansas! The sign traveled more than 30 miles.

In 1974, a chain of 148 tornadoes struck thirteen states. Scientists considered it a super tornado outbreak—the worst in U.S. history. In fewer than twenty-four hours, the tornadoes damaged more than 2,500 miles of land. More than 5,000 people were injured, and 330 died.

Luckily, this type of tornado outbreak is extremely rare. But even weak tornadoes can be dangerous and cause damage, so it's important to be prepared for them.

Staying Safe

One of the scariest things about tornadoes is that they are nearly impossible to predict. Sometimes, the weather conditions may be just right for a tornado to form, but then it doesn't. Experts want people to be prepared, but they don't want people to panic. So first, they watch and

Tornado sirens are used to warn people of an approaching tornado.

A single tornado can cause millions of dollars of damage.

monitor the data carefully. Meteorologists, scientists who study Earth's atmosphere, look at a variety of information, such as temperature and wind speed. They use tools like radar and satellite images to detect the movement of air in a storm.

Safety measures can save lives when a tornado happens. When experts spot a tornado or believe one is about to form, they issue a tornado warning. The warning tells people in the area to get to a safe spot right away. What is a safe spot? You're safest in the basement or the lowest floor of a strong building. You should stay away from windows, and if you're in a car, you should get out. It's best to get underneath something sturdy like a table, or to get into something like a bathtub that can protect you. Your family and school should have an emergency plan, and you should listen for tornado warnings on the radio or TV. If you hear one, take cover right away!

SUMMARIZE When you summarize, you tell the main ideas of a passage in your own words. A partial summary of this passage might be: *Tornadoes are dangerous storms. They form when winds blowing in opposite directions are forced upward, forming a spinning column of air. Tornadoes can be very destructive. They are hard to predict.* What is the main idea of paragraph 9? How would you add that to the summary to make the summary complete?

Comprehension Check

In "Nature's Worst Storms," the author explains how powerful tornadoes are, the destruction to property and human life they can cause, and safety rules people can use to protect themselves from them. What reasons and evidence does the author provide to support these ideas? The ideas are listed below. Fill in reasons and evidence that support each idea.

Ideas	Reasons and Evidence
1. Tornadoes are powerful storms.	a. Tornado winds can spin up to 300 miles per hour. b.
2. Tornadoes destroy property and human life.	a. b.
3. Following safety rules can help people protect themselves.	a. b.

Vocabulary

Use the word map below to help you define and use one of the highlighted vocabulary words from the Share and Learn reading or another word your teacher assigns you.

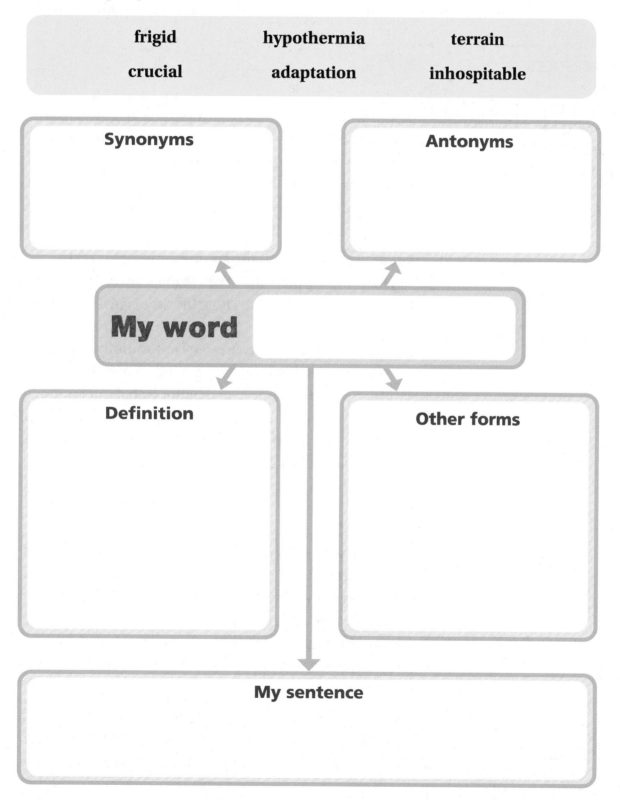

frigid hypothermia terrain

crucial adaptation inhospitable

Synonyms

Antonyms

My word

Definition

Other forms

My sentence

Consider ▶ What makes Antarctica a special place?

What special equipment do you think a scientist would need to study Antarctica?

Adapting to Survive

MAKE INFERENCES
Think about the weather conditions the author describes in Antarctica. Why do you think no scientist lives permanently in Antarctica?

Welcome to the Desert

1 Would you like to visit Earth's largest desert? If so, you need to pack differently than you might think. The driest place in the world is the continent of Antarctica. The reason it is so dry is because its weather is too cold for rain! Antarctica is also the coldest and windiest place on Earth. You'd better bring a parka, because this desert is frigid!

Antarctica is located at the southernmost part of the globe, surrounding the South Pole. A thick sheet of ice covers most of the continent's land. Huge blocks of ice float in the chilly water at its edges, and the mountains of Antarctica are covered in snow and ice. The ice isn't smooth enough to skate on, though, because strong winds have carved ridges into the surface. And you'd better watch out for the whiteouts. Whiteouts are scary weather conditions that occur when the wind picks up and blows large quantities of snow. The snow can be so thick that it is impossible for people to see anything but white!

A Lonely Place

Scientists who visit Antarctica stay there for long periods of time to study this unique environment, or habitat. No one lives there permanently, though, and the only housing is in scientific bases. No trees and few plants can survive the harsh conditions there, either. However, some animals, such as penguins, seals, whales, and squid, make their homes near or in the surrounding seas.

What *do* you need to pack if you're going to Antarctica? You'll be living at a base, a place where scientific research is done. This means that a lot of your supplies, such as food,

Some of the most extreme weather conditions on the planet are found in Antarctica.

tents, and medicine, will already be there. Extreme weather conditions can make it difficult for anyone to get to the continent, so there are extra supplies nearby. They are there so you'll be able to survive for more than a year if the base burns down or gets destroyed, and no rescue teams can reach you.

5   You will need to wear many thin layers of clothes. These layers should be made of fabric that dries quickly or is waterproof. Jackets, boots, gloves, socks, and hats should be waterproof as well. If you are wearing something that gets wet, it could freeze—and then, so could you! Then you could suffer from hypothermia. If this happens, your body will lose heat faster than it can produce it, and your heart and other organs won't be able to function correctly. In this case, your body will have to be warmed back to a normal temperature. And that could be difficult if you're out exploring the icy terrain.

You'll have to be especially careful to protect your extremities. Your hands, feet, and the body parts that are farthest from your torso can develop frostbite. Frostbite is a dangerous condition in which the skin and the tissues underneath it freeze.

There's one thing you will need that is something you would pack for any desert trip—sunscreen! The sun's rays are powerful, and the ultraviolet (UV) radiation from these rays can damage your skin. There aren't any trees on Antarctica to provide shade, so the only way to protect yourself from the sun is with a strong sunscreen and sunglasses or goggles.

> **PROBLEM AND SOLUTION** What potential problems does the author describe in this section? What solutions does the author offer?
>
> _____
>
> _____
>
> _____

MAKE INFERENCES
The author does not say how much time a scientist might spend on a field trip exploring Antarctica. Based on the author's description of the supplies needed, how long can you infer such a trip might last?

Heading Out

Now that you're ready to explore, you'll probably want to stay out in the field long enough to make observations and record your data. When you travel away from the base, you'll have to stay in a hut or a tent. You'll need to make sure that you have supplies that will last longer than you plan to stay, just in case you get stuck there.

You'll need a stove and lamp that are powered by wax. You'll also need an air mattress and a mat to sleep on, along with a special sleeping bag made just for the subzero temperatures of an Antarctic night. The food you bring should be packed with calories. Your body will be using a lot of energy to stay warm and to get from place to place. Of course, there won't be any restaurants or supermarkets where you can get more food. You won't need to bring water, though. There's plenty of freshwater in the snow and ice around you. You'll be fine as long as you have the tools and fuel to melt the ice and snow.

10   Finally, you'll need to be able to follow a plan, watch carefully, and pay close attention to your surroundings. All scientists need those skills, but in Antarctica, they are crucial. Scientists in Antarctica have to watch their subjects, but they also have to watch each other. It's important that they work as a team. This means constantly looking out for signs that show that someone on your team is in trouble.

Adapting to Antarctica

Scientists adapt to the extreme conditions of Antarctica by wearing special clothes and having detailed plans to help them survive when they go out. The animals they study, however, have naturally adapted to Antarctica's extreme conditions over millions of years. This makes Antarctica a great place for scientists to study how animals adapt and survive. They can also learn how animals on the land and in the sea depend on each other.

One Antarctic animal scientists study is the penguin. Each penguin species is unique, but they all share common features. Penguins have adaptations that help them survive in a place where other animals cannot. Their layers of fat, round bodies, and waterproof feathers help them stay warm.

Emperor penguins are the only penguins that live in the most extreme cold. They huddle together for warmth. They take turns moving from the outside of the circle (the coldest part) to the inside (the warmest part).

The male emperor penguin has a special fold in its stomach. This fold, or pouch, holds and protects an egg from the cold. The penguin also presses its feet against the pouch to keep the egg warm. The emperor penguin has adapted to the cold so well that it is one of only two animals that can survive the brutal Antarctic winter.

SUMMARIZE
Summarize how emperor penguins have adapted to life in Antarctica.

_____

_____

_____

DIAGRAMS Compare the diagram of the penguin with what you read in the text. What additional information does the diagram include? How does the diagram help you understand what the text says?

_____

_____

_____

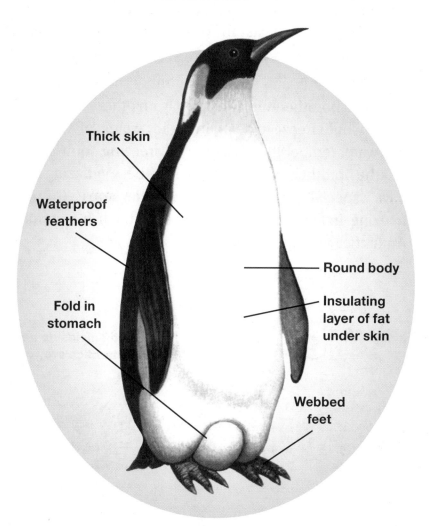

Thick skin

Waterproof feathers

Fold in stomach

Round body

Insulating layer of fat under skin

Webbed feet

15

SUPPORTING DETAILS
Weddell seals have adapted to be underwater hunters. Underline three details that tell about those adaptations.

SEQUENCE OF EVENTS
What happens after Weddell seals blow air into cracks in the ice?

_____

_____

_____

Another animal that is able to survive the inhospitable winters in Antarctica is the Weddell seal. These sea mammals spend most of their time underneath the ice. But they are mammals, so they still need to breathe air, just like you do. Weddell seals can hold their breath for twenty minutes while hunting underwater. They also memorize the location of holes in the ice and return to them to breathe in air. If they can't find a hole, they just use their sharp teeth to open one up. They wouldn't be able to hunt underwater if they had not adapted.

Weddell seals don't just use air to breathe, they also use it to trick fish and catch them. The seals blow air into cracks in the ice, scaring small fish that dart away. That makes it easy for Weddell seals to chase the fish and scoop up them up.

One fish the seals might meet under the ice is an Antarctic notothenioid. Most fish from other regions of the world would freeze to death in the icy waters of Antarctica. The water temperature is below the freezing point of blood. But the notothenioids do not freeze. These amazing fish have a special protein in their blood that stops it from freezing. In fact, about 95 percent of all the fish around Antarctica are notothenioids!

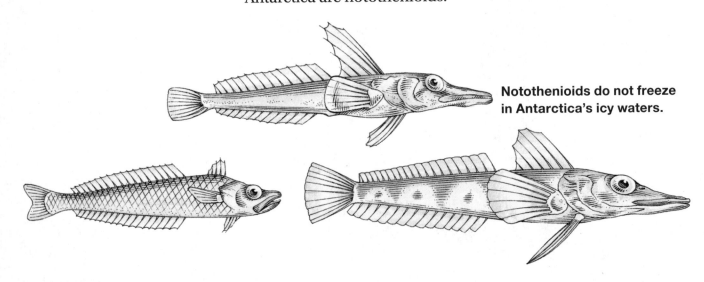

Notothenioids do not freeze in Antarctica's icy waters.

It's Feeding Time!

Antarctic Animals and What They Eat

Animal	What It Eats
Antarctic Krill	plankton (tiny, single-celled plants and animals that float in the sea)
Antarctic Cod	krill (a small shrimplike fish found in oceans around the world)
Squid	krill
Humpback Whale	krill
Polar Skua	krill, fish, and penguin eggs
Crabeater Seal	krill
Emperor Penguin	krill, fish, and squid
Fur Seal	fish and squid
Sperm Whale	fish and squid
Orca Whale	seals and penguins

CHARTS Which Antarctic animal eats the smallest type of food?

_____

Which Antarctic animal eats the largest type of food?

_____

SCIENCE VOCABULARY
Circle the words that help you understand the meaning of the word *krill*.

Few animals can survive in the harsh environment of Antarctica. The animals that live there depend on each other for survival. Antarctic animals do not have many choices about which other animals they can hunt for food. Many animals in this region depend on the tiny, shrimplike creatures called krill. Whales, seals, penguins, and seabirds all eat krill as the main part of their diet, eating between 150 and 300 million tons of krill every year. It's like the peanut-butter-and-jelly sandwich of the Antarctic animal world!

In addition to depending on each other for food, some animals depend on others for shelter. Most insects that live in Antarctica, for example, make their homes in the feathers and fur of birds and seals. There, the insects are protected from Antarctica's fierce winter climate.

20   Every year, scientists take more and more expeditions to the continent of Antarctica. Some scientists head there to study animals. Others research the layers of ice that give clues about Earth's history and changing climate. Others collect information about ocean currents. But they all have one thing in common: they know that there is much more to be discovered about this unique and fascinating place.

Many Antarctic animals eat krill to survive.

Anchor Standard Discussion Questions

Discuss the following questions with your peer group. Then record your answers in the space provided.

1. The author of "Adapting to Survive" describes krill as "the peanut-butter-and-jelly sandwich of the Antarctic animal world." What point is the author trying to support with this statement? Is there a more accurate comparison the author could have made? Support your response with details from the text.

2. Despite millions of years of physical adaptations, emperor penguins still have to huddle together to survive extreme conditions. How do humans depend on each other for survival in times of trouble? Cite examples from both texts to support your answer.

Comprehension Check

1. Which adaptation of the emperor penguin do you think would make it hardest for these penguins to live in a warm climate? Explain your answer.

2. What characteristics do you think a scientist who travels to Antarctica needs to have?

3. The number of people who visit Antarctica each year has grown from just a few hundred in the 1950s to more than 30,000. Do you think this is a good or a bad thing for the continent? Explain your answer with details from the text.

Read On Your Own

Read another scientific text, "Your Brain," independently. Apply what you learned in this lesson and check your understanding.

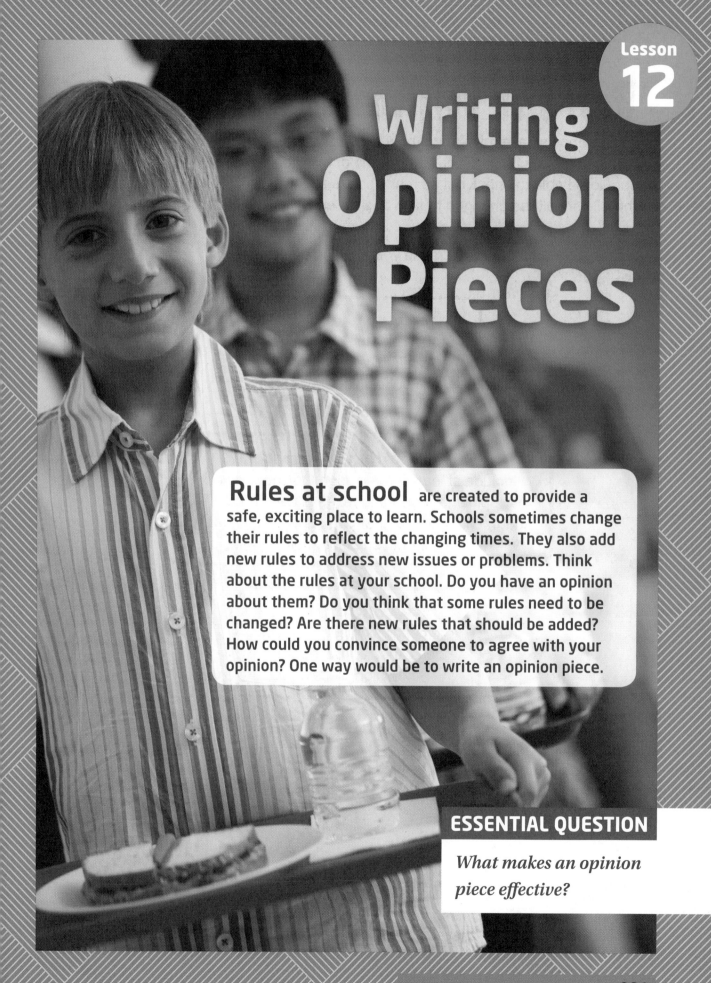

Writing Opinion Pieces

Rules at school are created to provide a safe, exciting place to learn. Schools sometimes change their rules to reflect the changing times. They also add new rules to address new issues or problems. Think about the rules at your school. Do you have an opinion about them? Do you think that some rules need to be changed? Are there new rules that should be added? How could you convince someone to agree with your opinion? One way would be to write an opinion piece.

ESSENTIAL QUESTION

What makes an opinion piece effective?

What's an Opinion Piece?

Many schools have rules about how many books students can check out of the library in a week. Maybe you think a limit of two books is fine. Maybe you think you should be able to check out as many books as you want. Or, maybe you think that the rule should be changed to four books per week. These are all opinions.

In an **opinion piece**, you tell about your opinion and try to persuade others to agree with you. Read the ways to make your opinion piece effective.

Your Opinion
State your opinion clearly. It should tell your readers exactly how you feel about a topic.

Supporting Reasons
Include at least three reasons to support your opinion. Supporting reasons can include judgments and facts. Strong supporting reasons will make your opinion piece more convincing.

A Conclusion
Your conclusion sums up your ideas and completes your opinion piece.

Let's look at an opinion piece.

Analyze a Mentor Text

This is an example of an effective opinion piece by a fourth grader. Read it and then complete the activities in the boxes as a class.

Vacation Should Be for Vacation: No More Vacation Projects!

What do you think when you hear the word <u>vacation</u>? Maybe you think about a time when you slept in late or went on a trip. When I hear the word <u>vacation</u>, I think of class projects that my teachers have assigned. I always have a big project due when I get back to school. Thinking about and working on these projects ruins my vacations. I think that assigning school projects during vacations should be banned.

Vacations should be a time for kids to get rest. Research shows that people of all ages do their best work when they are well rested. If you've had enough sleep, your brain is more open to learning new things.

Another reason is that kids need time to just play with other kids. Play can be very useful. For example, when my friends and I play, we work out the rules of games and interact with each other. These activities help us learn social skills that will help us become successful as we grow older.

OPINION
The writer gets the reader's attention in the introduction. The writer also states an opinion about completing school projects during vacations. Draw a box around the opinion.

SUPPORTING REASONS
The writer gives reasons that support the opinion in the second and third paragraphs. Underline the reason in each paragraph.

Vacations should be spent with family. Both my parents work hard. Both have to prearrange their schedules in order to take time off during my school vacations. If I have to work on projects, we can't have fun together.

In conclusion, I leave you with one last idea. If a project is worth doing, it is worth doing when you're in school. Vacations should be for resting, playing, and spending time with our families. When we get back to school, we'll all be ready to work together and learn more!

Think About It ▶ Who do you think the author had in mind while planning this opinion piece?

Do you think the reader is likely to be persuaded by the opinion piece? Why or why not?

Vocabulary Study: Latin Prefixes

A **prefix** is a word part that is attached to the beginning of a word. A prefix changes the meaning of the word. Many prefixes used in English come from the Latin language. The chart below identifies some common Latin prefixes and their meanings. Work with your class or a partner to fill in the blank boxes with words using each prefix.

Prefix	Meaning	Word with Prefix
extra-	outside, beyond	extraordinary
inter-	between, among	
pre-	before	
post-	after	
super-	above	

Look back at the opinion piece on school vacations on pages 233–234. Find two words with prefixes, and complete the chart below. Use a dictionary to check each word's meaning. Then write your own sentence using the word that shows the word's meaning.

Word
Prefix
Meaning

Word
Prefix
Meaning

Writing Process

Now that you have read and analyzed an opinion piece, you are going to create your own by following these steps of the writing process.

1. Get Ready: Brainstorm List topics you might want to write about. Choose the topic that you have the strongest opinion about. Think of reasons that support your view. Choose the strongest reasons for your opinion piece.

2. Organize Use a graphic organizer to organize supporting details and plan your work.

3. Draft Create the first draft of your opinion piece.

4. Peer Review Work with a partner to evaluate and improve your draft.

5. Revise Use suggestions from your peer review to revise your opinion piece.

6. Edit Check your work for spelling, punctuation, and grammar errors.

7. Publish Create a final version of your opinion piece.

Writing Assignment

In this lesson, you will write your own opinion piece. As you create the piece, remember the elements of the mentor text that were the most effective. Read the following assignment.

> Think about the rules and policies, or ways of doing things, in your school. Is there a rule or policy that you think should be changed? Is there a new rule or policy that you think should be added?
>
> Write three to five paragraphs telling your opinion about the rule or policy that you think should be changed or added. Be persuasive!

1. Get Ready: Brainstorm a Topic

The first step in writing an opinion piece is to choose your topic. Begin by listing several school rules or policies that you have strong opinions about. For each one, write reasons why you think the rule or policy should be changed or added.

Here's how the author of the mentor text brainstormed topics.

only two books per week from the library	class projects during vacations	field trips
I can read faster than that.	Projects ruin our vacations.	We have too many that are boring.

Try It!   Use a Brainstorming Graphic Organizer

Now use the chart below to help brainstorm topics for your own opinion piece. Choose the topic you feel most strongly about.

Brainstorm Ideas for Your Topic

You can use a graphic organizer to help brainstorm ideas and details for your opinion piece. Here is how the author of the mentor text used the graphic organizer.

OPINION Begin by stating your opinion clearly and strongly.

REASONS Give reasons that support your opinion. You may add to or revise your reasons as you draft your opinion piece.

DETAILS Now is the time to think of details that help explain your reasons. You will probably think of more details as you draft your opinion piece.

Opinion
School projects during vacations should be banned.

Reason
Kids need rest during vacations.

Reason
Vacation should be a time to be with family.

Reason
I want to play with friends during vacations.

Details

Details

Both my parents work hard.

We play games together.

They try to take time off during vacations.

By interacting, we learn social skills.

Try It!

Use a Graphic Organizer for Brainstorming

Now use the idea web below to brainstorm your opinion, reasons, and details for your own opinion piece.

Opinion

Reason

Reason

Reason

Details

Details

Details

2. Organize

You are almost ready to begin a draft of your opinion piece. You can use a graphic organizer to help organize the ideas and details you gathered during brainstorming. You can then refer to the graphic organizer as you work through the different parts of your draft. The writer of the mentor text completed this graphic organizer.

INTRODUCTION
In the first paragraph, you
- tell the topic of your opinion piece
- state your opinion about the topic

SUPPORTING PARAGRAPHS
In the second, third, and fourth paragraphs, you
- give a reason that supports your opinion
- elaborate on the reason with facts, experiences, and details

CONCLUSION
Your conclusion should
- briefly summarize your reasons
- add any new ideas to appeal to your reader

Opinion
School projects during vacations should be banned.

Supporting Reason 1
Vacations should be times for kids to rest. We're tired from having to get up early every day.

Supporting Reason 2
Another reason is that kids need time just to play. For example, games and sports help us develop good social skills.

Supporting Reason 3
Families should be able to spend time together. My parents work really hard. In addition, both try to take time off during school vacations.

Conclusion
During vacations, we should rest, play, and spend time with our families.

We can work on projects when school starts.

Try It!

Organize Your Opinion Piece

Now use the graphic organizer below to organize the ideas and details you want to use in the different paragraphs of your draft.

Opinion

Supporting Reason 1

Supporting Reason 2

Supporting Reason 3

Conclusion

3. Draft

Now it is time to begin the first draft of your opinion piece. Remember, your draft does not have to be perfect! This is the time to use your notes, get your ideas down in some sort of organized way, and have fun. You will have time to revise your writing later. Start by drafting your opinion piece on a computer or on a separate sheet of paper. Give your opinion about the rule you want to change or add.

Writer's Craft: Using Linking Words and Phrases

Linking words and phrases help writing flow smoothly. They also help readers understand how ideas are connected. Here are some common linking words and phrases.

Linking words	after, also, although, because, before, first, furthermore, finally, next, then
Linking phrases	even though, as long as, in addition, the first reason, the most important reason, another reason

The author of the mentor text uses linking words and phrases in his third paragraph.

LINKING PHRASES
Read this section of the mentor text. Circle the linking phrase that introduces a supporting reason. Underline the two sentences that the phrase "For example" connects.

Another reason is that kids need time to just play with other kids. Play can be very useful. For example, when my friends and I play, we work out the rules of games and interact with each other. These activities help us learn social skills that will help us become successful as we grow older.

Try It! Write Your First Draft

On a computer or a separate sheet of paper, complete the draft of your opinion piece. Remember to use linking words to connect your ideas. Use this drafting checklist to help you as you write.

✓ A good beginning gets your reader's attention. You can begin with a question, a quotation, or an interesting or funny experience.

✓ Be sure to state your opinion in the first paragraph.

✓ Write a topic sentence that clearly states the reason in each supporting paragraph.

✓ Use the reasons and details you wrote during Step 2: Organize.

✓ In each supporting paragraph, include sentences with details, facts, and experiences.

✓ Sum up your reasons in the end. Try to write an ending that your readers will remember.

Tips for Writing Your First Draft

- Write down key phrases and ideas before you begin writing. Sometimes this is a great warm-up to get you started!

- Focus on ideas, not details. Since you will revise and edit later, you can fix the details then. In drafting, it's the ideas that count.

- Sometimes students write better after physical activity. If you get stuck, take a walk around the block!

4. Peer Review

After you finish your draft, work with a partner to review each other's drafts. Here is a draft of the mentor text. Read it with your partner. Together, answer the questions in the boxes. Then we'll see how the writer's classmate evaluated the draft.

INTRODUCTION
In his draft, the writer does not state his opinion clearly. Does he think all class projects should be banned, or just those assigned over vacations?

SUPPORTING PARAGRAPHS
The third paragraph could use some linking words and phrases to make the ideas clearer. Which linking word or phrase could you add to the first sentence? Which word or phrase could you add to the beginning of the third sentence?

CONCLUSION
The conclusion does not really sum up the writer's reasons. How would you sum up the writer's reasons?

An Early Draft

No More Vacation Projects!

All I think about on school vacations are the projects I have due when school starts again. I think school projects should be banned. I know I'd be a lot happier if we didn't have them over vacations.

Vacations should be a time for kids to get rest. If you've had enough sleep, your brain is more open to learning new things.

Kids need time to just play with other kids. Play can be very useful. My friends and I often have to interact to work out the rules of a game. Such activities help us learn social skills that will help us become successful as we grow older.

Vacations are also supposed to be times with your family. Both my parents work hard. Both take time off during my school vacations. If I have to work on projects, we can't have fun together.

In conclusion, I leave you with an idea. If a project is worth doing, it is worth doing when you're in school. When we get back to school, we'll all be ready to work together and learn more!

An Example Peer Review Form

This peer review form gives an example of how a classmate evaluated the draft of the mentor text shown on page 244.

The introduction states the topic in an interesting way.	You did a good job of *telling the reader the topic.*
The writer gives a clear, strong opinion statement.	You could improve your opinion piece by *writing a clearer opinion. The one you wrote is confusing.*
The writer supports the opinion with at least three strong reasons.	You did a good job of *giving three reasons.*
The writer uses interesting details to explain the reasons.	You could improve your opinion piece by *adding some details to the second paragraph to support your reason.*
The writer uses linking words and phrases to make the writing flow smoothly.	You did a good job of *using "in conclusion" in the last paragraph.*
	You could improve your opinion piece by *adding linking phrases such as* **Another reason** *and* **For example** *in the third paragraph.*
The writer includes at least one new idea to interest readers.	You did a good job of *giving the reader a new idea about projects.*
The conclusion sums up the supporting reasons.	You could improve your opinion piece by *adding a sentence that sums up your three reasons.*

Try It!　Peer Review with a Partner

Now you are going to work with a partner to review each other's drafts.
You will use the peer review form below. If you need help, look back at
the mentor text writer's peer review form for suggestions.

The introduction states the topic in an interesting way.	You did a good job of
The writer gives a clear, strong opinion statement.	You could improve your opinion piece by

The writer supports the opinion with at least three strong reasons.	You did a good job of
The writer uses interesting details to explain the reasons.	You could improve your opinion piece by

The writer uses linking words and phrases to make the writing flow smoothly.	You did a good job of
	You could improve your opinion piece by

The writer includes at least one new idea to interest readers.	You did a good job of
The conclusion sums up the supporting reasons.	You could improve your opinion piece by

Try It! **Record Key Peer Review Comments**

Now it's time for you and your partner to share your comments with each other. Listen to your partner's feedback, and write down the key comments in the left column. Then write some ideas for improving your draft in the right column.

My review says my introduction	I will
My review says that my supporting reasons	I will
My review says that my use of linking words	I will
My review says that my conclusion	I will

Write anything else you notice about your draft that you think you can improve.

5. Revise

In this step of the writing process, you work on parts of your draft that need improvement. Use the peer review form that your classmate completed to help you. You also use your own ideas about how to improve each part of your opinion piece. This checklist includes things to think about as you revise.

Revision Checklist

✓ Does my beginning catch the reader's interest? Do I state my opinion clearly?

✓ Do I use details, facts, and experiences to make my reasons clear and strong?

✓ Is my conclusion interesting? Have I summed up my reasons well?

✓ Do I use linking words and phrases to make the writing flow smoothly?

✓ Do I use precise language to make my ideas as clear as can be?

Writer's Craft: Using Precise Language

Precise language means words or phrases that are clear and exact. Using precise words makes your opinion piece clearer and more convincing. For example, instead of using the word *big*, you might use the word *gigantic*. Instead of the word *small*, you might use *tiny*. Now look at the mentor text for examples of precise language.

PRECISE LANGUAGE
Look at the word *successful* in the last sentence. Would *good* have been more or less precise in this sentence? Why?

> Another reason is that kids need time to just play with other kids. Play can be very useful. For example, when my friends and I play, we work out the rules of games and interact with each other. These activities help us learn social skills that will help us become successful as we grow older.

Try It!
Revise Your Opinion Piece

Replacing simple words with more descriptive or precise words is an important part of revising. Practice using precise language with the following paragraph. Replace each underlined word with a more precise, interesting word. Write your answers on the lines below the paragraph.

> I like field trips. They are good ways to learn new things. Last week, we went to an art museum. There we saw some big statues. We also saw some pretty paintings.

Replace *like* with _____

Replace *good* with _____

Replace *big* with _____

Replace *pretty* with _____

Writing Assignment

Now it's time to revise the draft of your opinion piece. Continue working on a computer or on a separate sheet of paper. Review the assignment, repeated below, and the revision checklist. Doing so will help you know that you have included everything you need.

> Think about the rules and policies, or ways of doing things, in your school. Is there a rule or policy that you think should be changed? Is there a new rule or policy that you think should be added?
>
> Write three to five paragraphs telling your opinion about the rule or policy that you think should be changed or added. Be persuasive!

6. Edit

After revising your opinion piece, you will edit it. When you edit, you read very carefully to be sure to find any mistakes in your writing. Here's a checklist of some things to look for as you edit.

Editing Checklist

✓ Did you indent each paragraph?

✓ Are all of your sentences complete? Does each have a subject and a verb?

✓ Did you begin each sentence with a capital letter?

✓ Does each sentence end with the correct punctuation?

✓ Have you used commas correctly?

✓ Are all of your words spelled correctly?

If you typed your draft, print it out so you can mark it up. You can use these editing marks to mark any errors you find.

⌐ Indent   ⌃ Add   ~~delete~~ Delete

This paragraph from the draft of the mentor text shows how to use editing marks.

⌐In conclusion, I leave you with this idea: If a project is

is worth doing, it is worth doing when your in school.

When we get back to school, we'll all be ready to work

together and lern more!

Language Focus:
Relative Pronouns and Adverbs

Relative pronouns are *who, whose, whom, which,* and *that*.

Relative adverbs include *where, when,* and *why*.

Relative pronouns and relative adverbs are used in dependent clauses. A clause is a group of words with a subject and a verb. A dependent clause is a clause that cannot stand alone as a complete sentence.

Relative pronoun examples:

> The girl <u>who screamed</u> is scared of bees.
>
> The ball <u>that we are using</u> belongs to Anna.
>
> These activities help us learn social skills <u>that will help us become successful as we grow older</u>.

In each sentence, the dependent clause is used as an adjective. Each dependent clause describes the noun that comes before it. For example, the dependent clause *who screamed* describes the noun *girl*.

Relative adverb example:

> The park <u>where we play</u> is on First Avenue.

In this sentence, the relative adverb *where* begins the dependent clause. The dependent clause is used as an adjective. It describes the noun *park*.

What do you think when you hear the word <u>vacation</u>? Maybe you think about a time when you slept in late or went on a trip. When I hear the word <u>vacation</u>, I think of class projects that my teachers have assigned. I always have a big project due when I get back to school. Thinking about and working on these projects ruins my vacations. I think that assigning school projects during vacations should be banned.

DEPENDENT CLAUSES
Read this section of the mentor text. Use the information on this page to underline two dependent clauses that describe nouns. Circle the relative pronoun or adjective.

Try It! Language and Editing Practice

Underline the dependent clause in each sentence. Then circle the relative pronoun or relative adverb that begins each clause.

1. I lost the report that I wrote.

2. This book, which I borrowed from you, is very interesting.

3. Tuesday was the day when I was sick.

4. I'm going to the library where I can read my book.

5. Jack, who is determined, is a good swimmer.

Now use editing marks to correct the errors in this paragraph.

Our school recess is only tweny minutes long. My friend, whom name is Clark, and I are not happy about this. we both think that all kids in are school need longer recesses. Don't you think so. A longer recess will not make us more tired. In fact, students where get to play more outside are more focused during class. Teacher says that Clark and I move around two much at that desk.

Try It!

Edit Your Opinion Piece

Now edit your opinion piece. Use this checklist and the editing marks you have learned to correct any errors you find.

[ ] Did you indent each paragraph?

[ ] Are all of your sentences complete? Does each have a subject and a verb?

[ ] Did you begin each sentence with a capital letter?

[ ] Does each sentence end with the correct punctuation?

[ ] Have you used commas correctly?

[ ] Are all of your words spelled correctly?

[ ] Have you used relative pronouns and relative adverbs correctly?

Editing Tips

- Read your writing aloud. This will help you discover missing words and awkward phrases. Ask yourself, "Did that sound right?"

- Listen carefully as you read for stops and pauses. Stops and pauses usually indicate the places where punctuation might go. Ask yourself, "Am I missing any punctuation?"

- Read your writing over at a slow pace at least two times. When reading for small details, one reading is not enough!

7. Publish

On a computer or a separate sheet of paper, create a neat final draft of your opinion piece. Correct all errors that you identified while editing your draft. Be sure to give your opinion piece an interesting title.

The final step is to publish your opinion piece. Here are some different ways you might choose to share your work.

- Read aloud your opinion piece to your class or to a small group of your classmates.

- Gather your opinion piece and the work of your classmates into a booklet.

- Create a bulletin board display with your opinion pieces.

- Create a poster, using your opinion piece and drawings or photographs from magazines.

- Write a letter to the editor of the local newspaper.

Technology Suggestions
- Upload your opinion piece onto your class or school blog.
- Print out your opinion piece using decorative borders or paper.

Writing Handbook

A Guide to Functional Texts

Functional texts are things you read and write to help you in your day-to-day life. If you need to cook something, you read the recipe first. If you are going to a special event, you read the invitation to find out when and where the event will be. If you plan a party, you write invitations with the details. In this section, you will find examples of different functional texts and labels that show you the important features of each text. If you are asked to read or write one of these functional texts, use the sample in this handbook as a model to follow.

Models

On the top left-hand corner of the envelope, write your name, street address, city, state, and zip code.

Put a stamp on the top right-hand corner of the envelope.

Sender's name
Street Address
City, State Zip code

Recipient's Name
Street Address
City, State Zip code

In the middle of the envelope, write the recipient's name, street address, city, state, and zip code.

Scott Mester
12 White Knoll Drive
Pleasantville, NY 12345

Carolyn Long
34 Church Road
Old Bridge, Michigan 45678

Write your address at the top of the letter.

347 Elm Street
Baton Rouge, LA 70801

Include the address of the person to whom you are sending the letter.

Include the date.

March 4, 2012

Mr. Frederick Wright
959 Canal Street
New Orleans, LA 70111

Address the person you are writing with a formal greeting, including any appropriate titles, such as "Mr." or "Ms."

Dear Mr. Wright:

The body paragraphs of your letter should be well organized and clear. Be sure to maintain a formal tone.

Thank you for responding to my letter. I have not had a chance to read your new book. It will have to wait until school is over. Thank you for answering my questions. Your answers were very helpful. I received an "A" on my assignment. My teacher said she was impressed. She had never seen so many facts and information about your book.

My new assignment is about jungle cats. My teacher gave us a list of topics to research. I chose jungle cats. I read different sources in the library. They gave me a lot of information about jungle cats. You mentioned that you went to Africa in your last letter. Did you see any jungle cats?

Remember that your closing should match the overall tone of the rest of the letter. "Regards" and "Sincerely" are good choices.

Sincerely,

Andrew Walker
Andrew Walker

Sign your letter. Under your signature, type your first and last name so there will be no confusion about the spelling of your name.

Friendly Letter

Write your address at the top of the letter. Include the date.

582 Elm Street
Springfield, MA, 01152
January 5, 2012

The greeting should say "hello" to the person to whom you are writing. A comma should follow the greeting.

Hi Veronica,

What's up? How are you? I'm so glad you came out to visit last month. My mom says hi. Next time, I want to visit you. I've never been to New York. It sounds so fun. I want to go to the museums. I also want to see a musical. You're so lucky!

The body of the letter contains the main text or message. Each paragraph should be indented.

I know we haven't talked in a while. I've been so, so busy with school. Mrs. Nelson gave us such a hard assignment. I've been living in the library. I have to look for so many sources. And all I can write are facts and examples. Can you imagine?

Well, sorry I can't write a longer letter, but I have to get back to the library. I hope you are well.

The closing should say "good-bye." A comma follows the closing.

Your friend,
Sara
Sara

Sign your letter.

258

Start by providing the reason for the event.

Bill Cashman is celebrating his tenth birthday!

* **10** *

Join us as we celebrate on
Saturday, May 19, 2012 at 2:00 p.m.

Funtown Arcade
22 Middle Road
Springtown, Oregon

Regrets only to Mr. and Mrs. Cashman (123) 456-7890.

Include the date and time of the event.

Provide the location's name and address.

Provide a way for your guests to respond to the invitation.

Hello Mr. Dockery,

Please excuse Kevin from school for the week of November 12 to November 16. He has been diagnosed with chicken pox, and his doctor has recommended that he stay home to rest during his recovery.

Please send any available homework that he can complete during his illness, and Kevin will make up any work that he has missed when he returns to class.

Sincerely,

Robyn Sayre

Robyn Sayre

Peanut Soup

Ingredients:

The title of the recipe tells you what dish you are preparing.

- ¼ cup unsalted butter

- 1 medium onion, finely chopped

- 2 celery stalks, finely chopped

- 3 tablespoons flour

- 8 cups chicken stock

- 2 cups creamy peanut butter

- 1 ¾ cups light cream

- salted peanuts, chopped

The list of ingredients tells you what items you need to prepare the dish and how much of each item to use.

The instructions tell you how to prepare the dish and what cooking methods you should use.

Instructions:

1. Chop the onion, celery, and peanuts separately and place them in individual bowls while you melt the butter in a saucepan over medium heat.

2. Once the butter is melted, add the onions and celery and cook for about 5 minutes, until softened. Stir often.

3. Stir in flour and cook for 2 minutes.

4. Increase heat and add chicken stock. After you bring mixture to a boil, reduce heat and cook until thickened (about 15 minutes).

5. Strain over a bowl. Squeeze the vegetables to contribute as much flavor to the soup as possible. Then pour the soup back into the saucepan.

6. Whisk the peanut butter and cream into the soup for about 5 minutes over low heat.

7. Garnish with peanuts and serve warm.

Yield: Makes about 10 servings.

The yield tells you how many servings the recipe will provide.

Provide a title for the procedure.

Crayon Blackout

Do you want something wonderful and exciting to do on a rainy day? If so, this is the perfect art project for you! When you first begin to make a crayon blackout, your artwork might not seem that interesting. But in the end, you will be surprised. You will have a beautiful work of art to brighten up any day.

List all the materials needed to complete the procedure.

Here is what you'll need:

- paper (computer paper or drawing paper)
- crayons
- newspaper
- popsicle sticks, forks, toothpicks, or combs
- tape (optional)

Here are the steps for creating a crayon blackout:

Step 1 Find a large, flat workspace, such as a table or the floor. Place sheets of newspaper over your whole work area.

Step 2 Pick out a piece of computer paper or drawing paper.

Number each of the steps consecutively so that the reader can easily follow the order.

Step 3 Color all over your paper. Use as many colors of crayons as you like. Be sure to cover the entire piece of paper.

Step 4 Color over what you have done in black crayon. This can take a little time. Your hand might slip off the paper. That's OK! The newspaper is there to protect the floor or table. Take your time, and be sure to color your entire paper with black crayon.

Step 5 Scrape off parts of the black crayon to reveal the rainbow of colors underneath. To do this, pick a tool (a popsicle stick, a fork, a toothpick, or a comb). Scrape across your paper lightly. You want to take off only the black crayon. You want to leave the colorful crayon marks on your paper. Be careful not to tear your paper.

Step 6 Anywhere you scrape will reveal bright colors. So, use your imagination, and create wild designs!

Step 7 When you are done, you will have a rainbow of colors showing through the black crayon. You can use tape to hang your artwork on a window. When the rain ends, the bright sun will make your artwork glow!

Write a short introductory paragraph explaining what the experiment will be testing.

List all the materials needed for the experiment.

How Hard or Soft?

All rocks are made up of a combination of two or more minerals. However, not all rocks are the same. Different rocks have different properties. A property is something you can observe. One property of a rock is its hardness, or how hard or soft it is. You can test for the hardness of a rock by following the instructions below.

1. Gather these materials:

   - glass plate
   - penny
   - nail
   - permanent marker
   - 4 different kinds of rocks
   - masking tape

2. Make a chart like this one:

Rock	Fingernail	Penny	Nail	Glass
A				
B				
C				
D				

3. Use the masking tape and marker to label the rocks A, B, C, and D.

4. Try to scratch each rock with your fingernail, the penny, and the nail. Were you able to leave a mark? Record your results on the chart by putting "yes" or "no" in each box.

5. Try to scratch the glass with each rock. Were you able to leave a mark? Record your results on the chart by putting "yes" or "no" in each box.

Which rocks were you able to scratch with your fingernail? Which rocks scratched the glass? Which rock is the hardest?

List all the necessary steps in the experiment. Number them consecutively so the reader can easily follow the steps. Be sure they explain exactly how to perform the experiment and do not contain unnecessary information.

Read the title at the top of the label.

List all items separately.

If more information is needed, use an asterisk (*) and provide the additional information later.

Remember to keep wording short. Space is limited, so only use the words needed.

Nutrition Facts
Serving Size 8 oz
Servings Per Container: About 3

Amount Per Serving

Calories 180	Calories from Fat 60

	% Daily Value*
Total Fat 6g	10%
Saturated Fat 1g	5%
Trans Fat 0g	0%
Cholesterol 5mg	2%
Sodium 75mg	3%
Total Carbohydrate 26g	9%
Dietary Fiber 5g	19%
Sugars 11g	
Protein 8g	

Vitamin A 60%	Vitamin C 70%
Calcium 8%	Iron 10%

*Percent Daily Values are based on a 2,000 calorie diet. Your daily values may be higher or lower depending on your calorie needs.

	Calories	2,000	2,500
Total Fat	Less than	65g	80g
Sat Fat	Less than	20g	25g
Cholesterol	Less than	300mg	300mg
Sodium	Less than	2,400mg	2,400mg
Total Carbohydrate		300m	375g
Dietary Fiber		25g	30g

Calories per gram:

Fat 9   Carbohydrate 4   Protein 4

The title of a time line will tell you what subjects the time line is explaining.

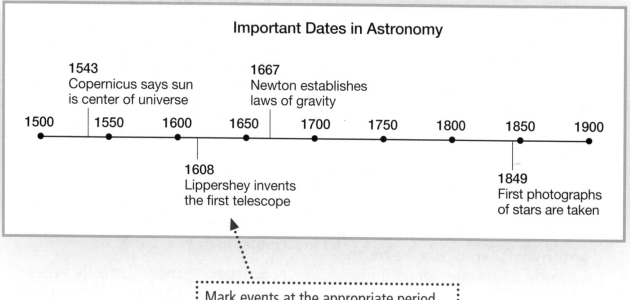

Important Dates in Astronomy

1543
Copernicus says sun is center of universe

1667
Newton establishes laws of gravity

1500   1550   1600   1650   1700   1750   1800   1850   1900

1608
Lippershey invents the first telescope

1849
First photographs of stars are taken

Mark events at the appropriate period along the time line. Call out dates, and provide a brief description.

Glossary

academic vocabulary specialized words used by people who study a certain subject or work in a particular field (Lesson 9)

adage an old familiar saying that expresses wisdom or a truth about human nature (Lesson 8)

adjective a word that describes a noun or a pronoun (Lesson 10)

affix a prefix or suffix that is added to a root word (Lesson 4)

allusion a reference to a well-known person, place, event, or piece of literature (Lesson 2)

antonym a word that means the opposite of another word (Lessons 5, 6)

ask and answer questions to ask and answer questions about key details in a passage and use the text to find the answers that will help you better understand what you are reading (Lesson 4)

cause a reason that something happens (Lessons 4, 9)

characters people or animals that take part in the action of a story (Lessons 1, 2, 3, 6, 8)

chart a graphic organizer that uses columns and rows to organize information; a title and headings tell what the chart is about and what type of information it includes (Lessons 9, 11)

chronological order the order in which things happen (Lesson 9)

comma a punctuation mark used to show a pause in a sentence or to connect ideas (Lesson 10)

compare to show the similarities between two ideas, people, places, events, or passages (Lessons 1, 4, 9)

complete sentence a sentence that contains a subject and a predicate (Lesson 3)

context clues words in a text near an unknown word that give clues about the meaning of the unknown word (Lessons 1, 2, 6, 7, 9)

contrast to show the differences between two objects, ideas, people, places, or events (Lessons 4, 9)

dependent clause a group of words that includes a noun and a verb but does not make sense on its own as a sentence (Lesson 12)

diagram a drawing with labels that shows the different parts of an object or how something works (Lessons 9, 11)

dialogue the words that characters say to each other (Lessons 3, 6)

dictionary a reference book that gives the meaning, the parts of speech, and the pronunciation of words (Lesson 3)

domain-specific vocabulary words that have a specific meaning in a particular kind of work or field of study, such as science, history, or technology (Lessons 9, 10)

drama a story that is performed on a stage by actors (Lesson 6)

effect a result of a cause (Lessons 4, 9)

fictional narrative a story that the author makes up (Lesson 3)

figurative language language that does not mean exactly what it says; it contains imagery or describes something through the use of unusual comparisons for added effect, interest, and meaning (Lessons 1, 7)

firsthand account a description of an experience or event that is told by someone who participated in the event described (Lesson 4)

formal language language used in school or business settings; words are usually carefully and accurately chosen (Lesson 8)

fragment a group of words that lacks a subject or a predicate (Lesson 3)

future progressive a verb tense that indicates an ongoing action that will take place in the future, such as *will be talking* (Lesson 8)

helping verb a verb used with another verb to indicate possibility, ability, impossibility, and necessity (Lesson 8)

historical nonfiction nonfiction text that tells about real events or people from the past (Lesson 4)

idiom a phrase that means something different from the literal, or dictionary, meaning of the words in it (Lesson 8)

informal language language used in everyday conversation (Lesson 8)

informative text nonfiction text in which the author presents information about a specific subject (Lesson 10)

linking words/phrases words or phrases that connect ideas to make writing flow better (Lessons 8, 10, 12)

make inferences to use information in the text and your own knowledge to figure out things that aren't stated directly by the author (Lessons 2, 4, 6, 7, 9, 11)

main idea the most important idea in a story or article (Lessons 4, 8, 9, 10)

map a picture that shows features, such as rivers, mountains, or streets, in an area; labels and a key tell about the information shown on the map (Lesson 9)

metaphor a kind of figurative language that compares two unlike things without using the word *like* or *as* (Lessons 7, 8)

meter the pattern of rhythm in a poem (Lesson 7)

mood the overall feeling created by a text (Lesson 7)

myth a story that explains something about the world; myths often involve gods or superheroes (Lesson 1)

opinion a personal belief that cannot be proven true (Lesson 12)

opinion piece a type of writing in which the author states a personal belief and tries to persuade others to agree (Lesson 12)

past progressive a verb tense that indicates a past action that was happening while another action was taking place, such as *was talking* (Lesson 8)

personal narrative a type of writing in which the author describes a personal experience (Lesson 5)

personification a kind of figurative language that gives human feelings and actions to something that is not human (Lesson 7)

plot the sequence of events in a story that includes the characters' actions, a conflict, and a resolution (Lessons 1, 2, 6)

poetry a genre of writing that is separated into lines and often stanzas, in which an author uses descriptive language and sometimes sound devices such as rhyme and rhythm to create meaning and call forth emotion in the reader (Lesson 7)

point of view the perspective from which a story is told; in the third-person point of view, a narrator uses the pronouns *he* or *she* to tell the story; in the first-person point of view, one of the characters tells the story using the pronoun *I* (Lesson 2)

precise language words or phrases that are clear and exact (Lessons 10, 12)

predicate the part of a sentence that tells what the subject does; the predicate contains a verb (Lesson 3)

prefix a word part added to the beginning of a word that changes the meaning of the word (Lesson 12)

preposition a word that links a noun or a pronoun to some other word in a sentence, often to indicate how things are related in time and space (Lesson 5)

prepositional phrase a phrase that begins with a preposition and ends with a noun or pronoun; can act as an adjective or adverb (Lesson 5)

present progressive a verb tense that indicates an ongoing action in the present, such as *am talking* (Lesson 8)

problem and solution a text organization in which the information describes a problem and then discusses a solution or solutions (Lessons 9, 11)

progressive verb a verb form used to express an ongoing action that doesn't have a specific end time (Lesson 8)

prose a form of writing in which one sentence follows another, with sentences arranged into groups called paragraphs (Lesson 6)

proverb an old familiar saying that expresses wisdom or gives advice (Lesson 8)

quotation marks punctuation marks used to show someone's exact words (Lesson 10)

relative adverb an adverb that introduces a relative clause, such as *when*, *where*, and *why* (Lesson 12)

relative clause a group of words that tells more about a noun (Lesson 12)

relative pronoun a pronoun that is used in a relative clause, such as *which*, *that*, *who*, *whom*, and *whose* (Lesson 12)

response to literature a type of writing in which the author describes and analyzes some aspect of a literary work (Lesson 8)

rhyme a sound device in which words end with the same sound; rhyme is often used in poetry (Lesson 7)

rhythm the beat, or pattern of sounds, in a poem (Lesson 7)

root word the base, or main part, of a word (Lessons 4, 10)

run-on one or more sentences run together without proper punctuation (Lesson 3)

science vocabulary words that have a specific meaning in a particular area of scientific study (Lesson 11)

scientific nonfiction nonfiction text that provides factual information and explains scientific events, procedures, ideas, or concepts (Lesson 11)

secondhand account a description of an experience or event told by someone who did not directly participate in the events (Lesson 4)

sensory language words that appeal to the five senses: hearing, sight, smell, taste, and touch (Lesson 3)

sequence of events the order in which events in a text happen (Lessons 5, 11)

setting the time and place where a story happens (Lessons 2, 3, 6)

short story a made-up tale with characters, a setting, and a plot that is usually short enough to read in one sitting (Lesson 2)

simile a kind of figurative language that compares two unlike things using the word *like* or *as* (Lessons 7, 8)

stage directions the words in a drama that tell actors what to do instead of what to say (Lesson 6)

subject the part of a sentence that tells what or whom the sentence is about (Lesson 3)

summarize to restate the most important ideas or information in a passage in your own words (Lessons 1, 2, 6, 11)

supporting details the facts or other information an author includes to support a main idea (Lessons 5, 8, 10, 11)

supporting reasons the details that support an opinion (Lesson 12)

synonyms words that have the same or similar meanings (Lessons 5, 6)

technical texts informative texts that explain events, procedures, ideas, or concepts; these texts explain what happens, why something happens, or how something works (Lesson 9)

text features items such as time lines, graphs, and captions that support the ideas stated in an informative text (Lesson 10)

theme the message about life or people that the author wants the reader to understand (Lessons 1, 2, 7)

time line a graphic that shows the dates when important things happened in a certain time period (Lesson 9)

topic the subject, or main idea, of a text (Lessons 10, 12)

transitional words/phrases words or phrases that connect ideas to make writing flow better (Lesson 5)

Acknowledgments

Picture Credits 5 Thinkstock; 20 (c) Thinkstock; 20 (l) Thinkstock; 20 (r) Thinkstock; 23 Thinkstock; 30 (l) Thinkstock; 30 (r) Thinkstock; 31 (l) Thinkstock; 31 (r) Thinkstock; 45 Thinkstock; 47 Shutterstock; 48 Thinkstock; 69 (full page) Library of Congress; 69 (inset) Wikimedia Commons; 70 Library of Congress; 72 Wikipedia; 73 Thinkstock; 74 (bg) Thinkstock; 74 (b) Wikipedia; 74 (t) Shutterstock; 75 Library of Congress; 76 (bg) Thinkstock; 76 Library of Congress; 77 Library of Congress; 80 NASA; 81 Thinkstock; 82 NASA; 83 NASA; 84 NASA; 87 Shutterstock; 89 Shutterstock; 90 Thinkstock; 111 Thinkstock; 129 iStockphoto; 130–131 Thinkstock; 132–133 Thinkstock; 145 Thinkstock; 147 Thinkstock; 148 (chest) Thinkstock; 148 (smoke) Thinkstock; 149 Thinkstock; 150 Thinkstock; 171 Thinkstock; 172 (l) Thinkstock; 172–173 Thinkstock; 174 Thinkstock; 176 Thinkstock; 177 Thinkstock; 180 Thinkstock; 181 Thinkstock; 182 Thinkstock; 183 (c) Thinkstock; 183 (l) Thinkstock; 183 (r) Thinkstock; 184 Thinkstock; 185 Thinkstock; 189 Thinkstock; 191 Thinkstock; 192 Shutterstock; 198 (b) Thinkstock; 198 (c) Thinkstock; 198 (t) Thinkstock; 215 Thinkstock; 216 (b) Thinkstock; 216 (t) Thinkstock; 218 Thinkstock; 219 Thinkstock; 223 Thinkstock; 225 Thinkstock; 226 (all) Thinkstock; 227 (all) Thinkstock; 228 Thinkstock; 231 Thinkstock; 233 Thinkstock; 234 Thinkstock.

Illustrations Cover Jing Jing Tsong; 6–9 Alida Massari; 10–13 Kali Ciesemier; 16–19 Maria Cristina Pritelli; 24–29 Alessandra Cimatoribus; 31–33 Dani Jones; 36–42 Natalia Vasquez; 71 Joe LeMonnier; 112–115 Judy Love; 116–119 Reggie Holladay; 122–126 Martina Peluso; 134–135 Gabhor Utomo; 136–137 Iva Sasheva; 140–141 Micha Archer; 142 Dani Jones; 173 William Graham; 174–175 Q2AMedia; 180 Joe LeMonnier; 181 Steve Stankiewicz; 198 Q2AMedia; 217 Q2AMedia.